The Doctor and the Dragon

The Doctor and the Dragon

Margaret Aitchison

Pickering Paperbacks

To my three step-brothers

Edgar, Robert and Tom,

all of whom

have been 'real' brothers to me

First published 1983
by Pickering & Inglis, 3 Beggarwood Lane, Basingstoke,
Hants RG23 7LP

ISBN 0 7208 0545 7

Text set in Garamond
Phototypeset by Input Typesetting Ltd, London SW19 8DR
Printed in Great Britain by Richard Clay (The Chaucer Press) Ltd,
Bungay, Suffolk

Contents

Prologue

A square-built, sturdy boy stood at the window of an upper room, gazing down at the bleak, rain-swept gables of the town of Greenock. It had rained all day, and water dripped from every eave, and every bare branch of every tree. It was beginning to get dark. It was Thursday, the 13th of November, 1879.

The boy was fingering a shiny new writing desk, installed in a little alcove by the window. On his face there was a look of mingled contrition, pride, and pleasure.

Presently he sat down at the desk, and wrote –

'God has spared me throughout another day. Oh! I am very ungrateful to God for his goodness to me. Yesterday, my birthday, I was to get another present from my mother and father, but by some mishap it did not come till today. I am writing on it just now. It was a splendid writing desk, furnished. It is a very handsome one, and I thank mother and father very much for it. My name is engraved on a small plate on the top. I have felt very well today.'

He paused, turned back the page of his black leather-bound diary, and looked at his entry for the previous day. In pure copperplate he had written –

'. . . got two scarfs, one from Maggie, and one from Edgar, a fine cake from my mother. I got three birthday cards sent to me. Growing sleepy. I have vowed myself to be GOD'S, with his help for ever.' Around the word 'GOD's', he hand inked-in a looped chain effect; and below that, right across the page, a series of thick strokes looking exactly like a rope.

Were the chain and the rope symbols of that tie which bound

him all his life to his God, in a bond which nevertheless freed him to seek out the wild isolation of Inner Mongolia, to live and work as a doctor in an area where, extending a thousand miles in every direction, no other doctor existed? And from there, to rebuild the hospital in Peking, demolished in the Boxer Rising, which was to become the first-ever training college in Western medicine for Chinese students? to become the only missionary ever to stand before the Dragon Throne; to become officially brother-in-law to the Dowager-Empress's favourite lady-in-waiting; and to receive visits from the Grand Eunuch, who came, like Nicodemus, only by night, and who was the dreaded power behind the dreaded Throne?

The boy closed his book, tidied his new desk, and left the room. He was thirteen years old. His name was Thomas Cochrane.

PART I

Mongolia

1

Journey into Mongolia

The Chinese junk lay at anchor on the eastern shore of the Gulf of Peichihli, with the waters of the Yellow Sea swirling around the hull. It was the season of storms, and the wind was rising.

As the two Europeans approached the junk, they thought it looked exactly like a huge Chinese coffin. Thirty five feet long from stem to stern, it was filthy, overloaded, and manned by a chattering Chinese crew who darted here and there like volatile yellow monkeys. The two travellers would have preferred to make this part of their journey by train, but in 1897 the Trans-Siberian railway was still in the future, and railway communications inside Manchuria were as yet only a blueprint.

These two, however, were not people to be deterred. Dr Tom Cochrane, short, dark, and handsome, was a thirty one year old graduate of Glasgow University. He wore a heavy black moustache, and had fine grey eyes. He had already known many hardships in his life. His invalid father had died when he was only 13, and Tom had been forced to leave school to help support his family. While still a boy, he had struggled with difficult and sometimes dangerous work in the Greenock docks by day, and with his school books by night. Driven by his determination to become a medical missionary, he had astonishingly gained admission to Glasgow University Medical School, where he qualified in 1896.

The girl by his side was slightly taller than Tom, and very upright in figure. She too was dark-haired and had large dark eyes. He had met Grace Hamilton Greenhill while she was nursing in a Glasgow Infirmary. They had married four months ago and sailed from

Southampton to Shanghai in January 1897. There they had experienced tedious and difficult delays. Then the Port of Tientsin was ice-bound for several weeks, which delayed them even further. So now it was April, and they had finally reached the last leg of their journey.

With the Cochranes stood their new Chinese friend and factotum, Lien-Yi, who had undertaken to get them safely to the town of Chaoyang in Southern Mongolia, their final destination. Lien-Yi surveyed with undisguised satisfaction the product of his bargaining, the filthy junk lying among scores of similar craft. He beamed, he was confident; yes, he had done well for his new Western friends.

In return, Tom Cochrane eyed him not without satisfaction. He had spent most of the previous day with Lien-Yi, who loved nothing more than to bargain. Lien-Yi wore a Chinese cap with a piece of fur on it, part of which hung down over his left eye. When the bargaining had reached a critical point, he had drawn the doctor's hand into his wide Chinese sleeve and had manipulated Tom's fingers to indicate how much money to offer. Nobody but Tom could see Lien-Yi's half-covered expressive eye or feel the coaxing fingers which told him when to clinch the bargain.

Tom stood now, gazing out over the desolate shore line. As far as the eye could reach, mud banks and creeks, creeks and mud banks, were all that could be seen, save that here and there masts were sticking out of the water, marking the places where junks had sunk. Two poles with a cross-bar from which a solitary paper lantern hung, seemed to Tom remarkably like a hangman's scaffold. He shivered in the early morning breeze.

His thoughts turned back to that day in London, in the Board Room of the London Missionary Society. He had been asked, 'Where would you like to go?' He had wanted above all things to go to the Sudan, but that door was closed. Now his answer was, 'To the neediest place there is!' So they had assigned him to Mongolia, to replace the famous and beloved missionary, James Gilmour, who had died six years earlier.

He reflected now not for the first time that James Gilmour would not be an easy man to follow. That intrepid adventurer had traversed Mongolia time and time again, learning to ride the fast Mongolian ponies, and sharing tents with lamas. He had even made his own tent, with an extra outer canopy to retain warmth in winter and keep out the burning sun in summer – an innovation admired but not copied by the jealous, suspicious Mongols.

This man, whose wife had died tragically of tuberculosis in Peking, had learned to share the hardships and the joys of the nomadic Mongolian tribes, and had learned to speak their language so fluently that he was accepted everywhere in Mongolia from China, in the south, to Russia in the north. Wherever he went, he took with him a simple medical kit which he used on a basis of instinct and commonsense, but with no medical training. Herein, thought Tom, lay the difference between them. He had come, with the avowed intent of devoting all the skills of his medical training, to bring a knowledge of God's love and light to these same people.

Tom had heard many stories of these ignorant, disease-ridden people who were a prey to superstitions and idol worship. He had heard of a man who travelled a hundred miles writhing on his belly, prostrating himself at every pagan shrine till he had calluses on his forehead; and of a boy whose mother was ill crawling from idol to idol with a heavy saddle on his back, and a skewer through his flesh, moaning as he went 'for my mother's sake.'

James Gilmour had died of typhus in 1891, and for six years there had been a void during which there was no one to bring hope or healing to the people of Mongolia. Tom wondered what his own reception would be.

His thoughts were interrupted by a sudden commotion on board, a tug on his sleeve by his wife, and nods and winks from Lien-Yi as he urged his friends to embark on the coffin-like vessel. As they went aboard, they both felt and feared it might be the only coffin they would ever have. They were pushed down a heavy plank into a tiny hold used either for cargo or for passengers, and lined with straw. It was impossible to stand upright in this space which was so narrow that two people lying down could only do so in each others' arms, and when they wanted to turn over it was only possible by mutual consent.

This tiny cell was to be the Cochranes' 'home' – though they did not know it then – for the next six days. They had been told the crossing would take twelve hours, but as soon as they sailed, a storm blew up which chased them from one side of the Gulf to the other, up muddy creeks for shelter where brigands lay in wait, and out to sea again only to encounter pirates who gave further chase. Many junks were sunk around them, but throughout most of this drama the Cochranes were battened down in the cramped airless compartment where sleep and rest were made impossible by the swarms of 'China's millions' – bedbugs which infested their straw palliasse and their clothing.

On the fifth day food and water ran out, and the sixth day was for them a day of prayer, whilst the crew began to burn incense to their idols. On the evening of the sixth day they staggered up on deck and surveyed the stark, ugly, ochre-coloured coast which was their destination. Tom thought wryly that theirs must surely be the strangest honeymoon that any couple could ever have.

'If there was any romantic element in my decision to become a medical missionary,' wrote Tom Cochrane years later, *'it vanished as I gazed disconsolately at the muddy shores of Manchuria and realised that as a foreigner there was no welcome for me there.'*

Manchuria, however, was not their final destination. Manchuria was on the way to Chaoyang, the 'City Facing the Sun' or the 'City of the Three Towers', as it was also called. Here James Gilmour had founded a small mission station in his latter days, where the Mongol tribes were mainly agricultural and had settled on the land around it. The city itself, however, was Chinese in character, and its inhabitants and language were nearly all Chinese. The Chinese and the Mongolians had little love for each other.

Tom and Grace disembarked, thankful again to breathe fresh air and to be quit of their louse-ridden cell. They were in fact merely exchanging one form of physical torture for another. A Chinese cart awaited them, a kind of dog kennel on wooden wheels and without springs. For four days they trundled over rutted roads, along dry river beds and sometimes narrow ledges with a sheer drop of hundreds of feet on one side. A further hazard was caused by little rat-like creatures who excavated galleries underground making hollows in the ground. Although the danger spots were distinguished by a different colour and appearance, they could, if not spotted, fell a horse and rider, or overturn a cart. Even on the first day of their cart journey, Grace looked increasingly white and spent, and she clutched her husband's arm every time they seemed to round a corner on two wheels. The motion of the cart was somewhat akin to that of a ship when the screw stops, but she wondered why it was that now they were on dry land she still had the deadly feeling of nausea.

Tom, however, did not seem to be suffering in the same way. He appeared if anything exhilarated by the 'near misses' and other risky habits of their driver who would never give way to an oncoming cart or rider, however narrow the road. The only thing which appeared to worry him was the persistent pounding of the pony's hooves, which became a pitiless scourge to his eardrums. At their first stopping place, he got out of the cart and examined the pny with great interest. He was puzzled by what distinguished it from the ponies he had known around his native Greenock. Then he saw that the tail, which was thick and surprisingly well-groomed, had been allowed to grow full length to the ground. He wondered if this was a general practice in Mongolia, but his command of the language was not yet good enough to be able to question their carter. Presently, however, his curiosity was satisfied, when their driver padded up to the pony in his cotton shoes, and plucked some of the long hairs from its tail. These he wove into a strong plait with which he was able to make a repair to a worn strap in the harness.

The Mongols were nothing if not resourceful, Tom reflected. At least, they knew how to survive. But did they know how to *live*? This was a totally different question to which he was soon to get an answer, as they made their weary way to their first inn.

A friend had told them that Chinese inns were places you could get bed and breakfast for twopence, but it was not worth it. To travellers who had been bumped and bruised from dawn to dusk, however, they held out the prospect of some comfort, however primitive. They were welcomed at their first night's stopping place by a dirty, unkempt inn-keeper who declared grandly that all the comforts of his unworthy hostelry were at their disposal.

The 'comforts' consisted of a mud-walled room with mud floor and mud roof, and the bed – or *kang* as it was called in Chinese – was simply a mud platform raised three feet from the floor. On this the Cochranes had to spread their own quilted bedding. 'Dinner' consisted of tea – the poorer Mongols were always short of tea, and theirs were tea 'bricks' composed of twigs and pounded leaves, on to which the inn-keeper poured boiling water with great ceremony. There followed two steaming bowls of dough strings and a small dish of fried bean curds flavoured with fragments of chopped mutton, greasy and unappetising. There was no choice, and hunger overcame even Grace's nausea. When finally they fell exhausted onto the *kang*, at least they did not have bedbugs for companions. They had fleas instead.

The countryside in Southern Mongolia consists of hills and plains, which have a dreary and desolate appearance in winter. The plains are brown, the mud houses brown, the trees brown and leafless. The bare brown hills are broken only by occasional villages. This was April, however, and every village now had its clump of green, the plains showing the first shoots of grain which in summer would grow much higher than European crops. Millet, in particular, grew to a height of eight foot, and brigands could actually ride through it on horseback, unseen by unwary travellers whom they pounced upon and attacked from behind. For this reason, in the future, Tom Cochrane was to adopt Chinese dress and wear a queue – a pigtail hanging down the back of the head – while travelling round the villages in the Chaoyang district. This was bandit-infested country, and foreigners were always at risk. The Mongols invariably suspected them of being spies.

One small incident during their journey brought home to the Cochranes their vulnerability as foreigners. The driver of their cart had a bad stammer. Quite naturally, they had been trying to practise their first words of Chinese on him. Most Mongols could speak or understand Chinese. Their hesitant and stumbling efforts had suddenly caused him to take offence. He thought they were mimicking him, and making him look a fool. He withdrew from them in a towering rage. The next morning, after their fourth and last night in an inn, they were informed by their inn-keeper that they no longer had a driver. He had walked out of the inn the night before, vowing he would have no more to do with the hated foreigners. A new driver appeared, however, more cheerful and smiling than the old one, and so thankfully they set out on the last stage of their journey.

They saw the castellated walls of the city far away on the horizon, and their new driver cracked his whip and shouted the only word they could fully understand, 'Chaoyang!' Soon they would be in the shelter of their new home, which they knew had been prepared for them by the small group of Christians who had been James Gilmour's devoted friends and followers. Soon they would be able to rest for a short time after their long journey from Scotland to this new, and to them, barbaric, country.

As they neared the city, Tom tried to make out what the tall poles were which were planted at intervals all around the city walls. Nearer still, he suddenly realised with horror that each pole was ornamented with a severed human head. Some were mere skulls which grinned at him in macabre welcome, others, freshly executed, had as yet merely had the eyes picked out by the swarms of buzzards and crows which circled overhead. The decapitated bodies lay all around on the ground, and were being systematically picked to pieces by these disgusting scavengers and by half-starved dogs. Worst of all, on top of a heap of City refuse by the gate, lay the body of a newly-born baby, half-eaten.

Tom leaned forward instantly, and drew the curtain which separated the passengers from the driver, obscuring the view. He was too late. As he turned to Grace she stared back at him with an indescribable look of mingled terror and incredulity. He tried to put his arm around her to draw her close, but with one convulsive, twisted movement, she turned from him, leaned out over her side of the cart, and was violently sick.

So they came to Chaoyang.

2

'Reality'

'*I stood at the door of our little Chinese bungalow, and romance, if there were any, merged into reality. I looked over the great plain shut in by encircling hills, and I became aware of an enveloping depression, as it came home to me that I was the only medical man in thousands of square miles of bandit-ridden territory, and that it would be as much as my life was worth if I should happen to perform an unsuccessful operation.*'

Had Tom allowed it, this depression would have deepened the day after their arrival, as he took stock of his environment and the premises awaiting them. It would have been hard to find anything more primitive or unsuitable than those in which he found himself in this Mongolian border town.

The living rooms were bad enough but the rooms allotted to him for medical work were worse. A mud wall surrounded such buildings as there were, over which thieves could climb at night. Eventually, Tom would be obliged to hire a night watchman to prevent petty thieving, but the watchman would often sleep, and thieves would be difficult to catch, as they greased their bodies and stuck needles into their pigtails.

There were two small rooms in which Tom could receive in-patients. Each had a mud floor, and there was only a *kang* – a mud platform raised about three feet in the middle of the floor – for patients to lie on. The *kang* was heated by means of flues, or spaces, through which flames and smoke from burning grain stalks passed, to emerge through a mud brick chimney. The windows in all the buildings were composed of six inch square apertures, pasted over by translucent paper. A reception room for patients was large enough to contain twenty or thirty at a time, provided some were lying or sitting on the floor, and the others on backless benches. This room communicated with the dispensary, adequate in size to accommodate half a dozen patients at a time. This was paved with broken bricks and lighted by thin white paper windows, through which came a dim light. The ceiling was made of grain stalks, papered underneath. Between the lime mud roof and this ceiling, rats played havoc, and were constantly in danger of falling through when the roof leaked and the paper became sodden. Occasionally one did fall through, and had to be immediately despatched. Hygiene was going to be a major problem, and bubonic plague was rampant, as Tom soon discovered. The thought of operating in these conditions appalled him, and the paucity of his equipment, the lack of assistance, and inadequate supply of drugs added to the demonic nightmare. He bemoaned the fact that he had come out to this – 'the neediest place there is!' – in such ignorance of the conditions in which he would have to work. Nobody had really given him reliable information, nor had pointed out the enormity of his task. 'Why wasn't I told?' he lamented to Grace. 'All this would have seemed marvellous to Gilmour, but it is a poor show to a doctor placed as I am.'

His wife looked at him stolidly. She was pale as a result of their terrible encounter the night before, but she had recovered her composure. She did not attempt to give her husband any comfort. 'Tom,' she said, 'You asked for the neediest place. Now you've got it.'

He relaxed, smiled at her, and said, 'Now I'm going out to discover what the rest of Chaoyang is like. You stay here and rest.' They knew now without a doubt that Grace was pregnant, and that the travel sickness had not been wholly due to the discomforts of their journey. As Tom walked out of the house, a full realisation of what he had committed himself and his young wife to, overwhelmed him. To this stinking city, to this wild, uncivilised people, so callous that they had strolled past the headless bodies the night before, without appearing even to notice them, he had come with the ambitious resolve that all of Mongolia could be evangelised in one generation. Given God's power and mercy, and his own gifts of medical training and skill, he would, in ten years of steady, uninterrupted work, prove to be the envoy of salvation to these rough, enigmatic people.

He paused at the opening of a little alley; was this in reality a presumptuous idea, or was it really God's plan and purpose for his life? He recalled his 13th birthday vow, but at that moment, a large black pig emerged from the side alley, and charged at him, so that he had to leap aside and let it go grunting and blundering past. Looking down the alley, he saw dismal little mud brick houses, a river of filth running in a stream between them, and mounds of excrement dotted here and there, around which were more black pigs, and fierce, wolf-like dogs, feeding on whatever refuse they could find. Accustomed as he was to the slums of Glasgow, he had never encountered, nor even imagined, anything as foul as this. Plague, cholera, typhus, typhoid, all and more of such diseases must surely breed in these conditions, as he was very soon to find out. He wandered around the town, estimating its population at perhaps fifteen thousand people, most of whom were Chinese because of its proximity to the border, but with a good sprinkling of Mongols. He noticed the huge lama temple which dominated the town, and the magistrates' *yamen* adjacent to it, which was of interest, not on account of its architecture or situation, but because it was the centre of officialdom – 'the courts of injustice,' as he found it was called by Chaoyang's inhabitants.

The Chaoyang Buddhist Temple was famous, and its buildings and courts covered a large area of ground. Inside the temple there were many idols scattered around the wall, but the place of honour was reserved for a huge image of Buddha before which a lamp was kept burning day and night. The rest of the building, however, was forbidding, dark, and tawdry. When Tom somewhat hesitantly entered, a religious service was in progress, but apparently only the priests attended, sitting in rows, their scalped heads bent over their chests as they muttered and mouthed incantations and chants in a language they clearly did not understand. From time to time, they rang bells and clashed cymbals as an accompaniment to their monotonous and sombre chants; but they appeared totally uninspired in their devotions which they did not seem to understand. Tom decided they were uncouth, dirty, ignorant men, whose vacant stare and low frontal development was repellent. At later visits to the lamasery, when he was called to give medical assistance or help, this first impression of ignorance and disease amongst its inmates was enhanced, particularly when he met the Head Lama, who displayed animosity and downright hostility to the foreign doctor who had dared to come on to his terrain, bringing ideas which were unacceptable.

As Tom turned and walked away, dismayed and disgusted by what he had seen, a priest passed him, and as he did so made a revolting gesture of contempt and rejection. He had an evil face, seam-lined, sullen and lowering, his eyes conveying a look of murderous dislike. As Tom emerged once more into the street, his wife's words came back to him. He had asked for the neediest place. 'Lord,' he said inwardly, 'unless you have something worse to show me, I think I have just seen the neediest people here.' He suddenly remembered Grace, whom he had left alone in the house, in this alien and hostile atmosphere, pregnant with his child, travel-worn and dismayed, as he was, but wholly supporting him. Without thinking he began to run, unaware that people were stopping to look at this mad foreigner who was in such haste. He arrived, panting, at the little house, to find Grace calmly sorting out the small equipment for the surgery which they had brought with them. 'Tom,' she said, 'I think you've just got your first patient.' She gestured towards the dispensary. A man was standing there, obviously nervous at finding himself inside the 'foreign devil's' house, anxiety written all over his face. He wore the clothes of a peasant of the plain; a blue cotton jacket, blue cotton trousers, white cotton socks, and black cloth shoes with felt soles. His queue was coiled around his head, but immediately he caught sight of the doctor, he uncoiled it, and let it fall down his back and then, getting down on his hands and knees, he thumped his forehead on the brick floor, saying, *'Taifu, chiu ming! Taifu, chiu ming!'* ('Doctor, save life! Doctor, save life!') Tom did not understand the exact meaning of the words, but he recognised a desperate plea for help. He was amazed at the attitude of respect displayed towards him by this man, so utterly different from the lama priest's. He quickly helped the man up on to his feet, and in an exchange of sign language, he understood that he was needed to help a woman in labour. He accompanied the man to the door and saw a cart awaiting them. In a few seconds, he had collected his medical bag, complete with bottle of chloroform, and within minutes they were on their way.

Still bruised and sore from his four-day journey by cart to Chaoyang, Tom prayed that it was not far to go. At length they came to a village, typical of so many villages scattered over the northern plains: a broad street, little mud houses in narrow lanes leading off it, filled with naked children sporting in muddy pools. Outside the door of one of these little houses stood a huge coffin. They had arrived.

The woman was lying dirty, dishevelled, and desperate, on a heap of earth on the *kang*. Tom realised she had been in labour for a long time, probably several days. Her state was indescribable. In a few seconds, he had given her a few whiffs of chloroform – the marvellous 'dream medicine' as the Chinese were to call it – and she was blissfully unconscious as he saved her life. The child was dead, mutilated by the dirty old hags who had misguidedly tortured the mother while trying to deliver her. He waited till she was conscious, and was rewarded by a gleam of gratitude in the eyes of a member of an alien race.

As he gathered his things together in that little mud house on the plains of Mongolia, the relatives kotowed to him, exclaiming, '*Taifu, hsinhao, Taifu, hsinhao!*' ('The Doctor's heart is good! The Doctor's heart is good!')

The sun was setting as he stood in the doorway, and as he waited for the cart, he mused upon the unrelieved anguish of women that there must be in a myriad of villages for whom there was no help available. He was the only doctor in thousands of square miles of territory. From what he had seen of the temple in Chaoyang, there would be no help forthcoming from that quarter. He felt that here was a nation waiting to be healed, and they knew nothing of the Great Physician. His heart suddenly lifted, and the certainty poured into him that this was why he had come. His previous depression, and the spiritual darkness which had descended on him after his visit to the temple dissolved into joy and lightness of spirit. He climbed back into the cart, and was driven back to Grace.

It was dark by the time he arrived back, to find she had expertly laid out all his medical equipment, and had finished unpacking their few personal possessions. She was also preparing some sort of a meal for them from the iron rations they had brought with them. Gratefully he sank down into a chair and described the miserable event in which had just taken part, thankful that his wife was a fully trained nurse from whom he did not need to conceal any of the horrible details.

Grace's eyes lit up with compassion and then anger, as she realised what the sufferings of this poor woman had been. Tom felt a sudden glow of comfort at the warmth of feeling in this wife of his who had so gladly agreed to share her life with him, and already was showing concern for all that involved them. He felt deeply that women were wonderful, and that his God had truly supplied his need of solace and support with exactly the right woman.

Should he have brought her here? For the second time that day, he had misgivings for her and for his unborn child. Then he pulled himself up. Faith required that he did not look back, and that he believed implicitly that 'all things work together for good to them that love God.' There was no doubt that they both loved God, and they loved one another.

They had made a pact, when they married, that they would never go to bed at night with any suppressed resentment or fear in their minds, or even unshared problems or doubts. They would always pray together, and read a Psalm or short passage from the Gospels. This was a resolution Tom was never to break.

As he lay in bed that night, trying to sleep in these strange surroundings, the events of the day passed before his vision as on a screen. Suddenly the leering face of the lama priest swam into his consciousness, close and threatening. He saw again the look of malevolence, spiteful and hideous. As he recoiled inwardly, he prayed, 'Lord, what could a man who looked like that possibly be like inside, what could he believe in? What can I do, what can I say to these people?' He had been repulsed; he had almost literally run away. What had he run from? He tried to think it out as sleep began to overcome him. Ugliness? Hatred? Yes, all of that and more. 'And man was made in the image of God, in his image God made him.' Then that man was of God's creation, and was loved by him. It seemed hard to believe. Another text came into his mind: 'The Son of Man came to seek and to save that which was lost.' Not the good, not the pious, but the trapped, the lonely, the deprived, even the perverted. As he sank into unconsciousness he prayed, 'Lord, help me to learn to love the unlovable.' He would never again run from a fearful spectacle. His last thoughts were, 'lost . . . that priest was lost . . . lamas are lost . . . lamas . . . lost . . . lost.'

In a minute, he was asleep.

3

Patients and Problems

The next morning Tom slid skilfully past Grace, who slept more heavily than he did, and resumed the practice which, after his thirteenth birthday, he maintained throughout his life, though the four months' journey to Mongolia had sometimes disrupted it. He had always carefully guarded the first precious hour of the day, which he spent alone, armed with his Bible and notebook. He referred to this at times as 'the place of thunder', at times as his 'Bethel.' It was during these times alone with God that he received the direction and the discipline of his life. He recorded in his diaries his deepest desires, his failures and his doubts and his sorrow for the sins of others and himself. He divulged his most intimate thoughts. These were personal, spiritual diaries, not intended, as he wrote them, for any eyes but his own.

Because of this habit, in life Tom never criticised anybody; he preferred, if possible, to keep his mouth shut. If it ever became necessary to disagree with, or remonstrate a fellow-worker, his wife, or even his children – let alone his 'enemies' in religion – he did so with a gentle and kindly persuasiveness that was usually completely disarming. However strongly he felt on any subject, he never raised his voice in anger, though his diary entry next day might reflect his struggles in prayer to find a solution to the practical problems of life, including his personal relationships.

As he dressed, shaved, and finally settled down to his favourite hour, all that now faced him rose to the surface of his mind. First, though, he recorded his delight in being reunited with his notebooks, which had travelled from Shanghai in packing cases, and now were back in his possession.

'*Bringing this dear old book to light after my long voyage and journey has given me such a lift spiritually . . .*' he wrote, and later, '*my Father, I want to walk in the Spirit, to be spiritually-minded, to have revealed unto me by close contact and constant communion . . . the deep things of God. How rare it is to find fully developed men in this direction.*'

Not only in the spirit, but in the flesh, too, he found relief in his prayer life as recorded in his diary. When Grace's confinement drew near, and he realised that he himself would have to be her obstetrician, he described her condition and debated the wisdom of using chloroform in his notebook. Deciding on August 10th that he would not undertake certain treatment in advance of her delivery, he wrote, '*My Father, I think it better to leave it to Thee to do the best for me. I know what Thou hast done and been in the past. Let me have this also, to praise Thee for, my God.*'

In the event, Edgar was born on the 21st day of September, a big, energetic baby, with long legs and a strong frame, and with thick black hair. His eyes soon turned from dark baby blue to near-black. He resembled his mother entirely, his father not at all. Those Chinese and Mongols who had become their friends were delighted, and claimed that he deserved to be one of them.

But it was still May, 1897, and these events lay ahead. During his morning hour, that second day in Chaoyang, Tom decided that he had to act quickly in all that he did. First, there was the question of language. He had to acquire a working knowledge of this as fast as possible. Then there was the question of an assistant. He could now no longer rely on Grace for help in his dispensary on a regular basis, as had been his original hope. Next, they must organise some sort of domestic routine and teach a Chinese to cook and help with the affairs of their small bungalow, and be ready to take charge temporarily when the baby was born.

Lastly, there was the question of the inadequacy of their premises. When James Gilmour had died, he had left behind this small and insignificant little Chinese bungalow, and the bizarre and apparently purposeless collection of rooms which neither constituted any known sort of a building, nor, in Tom's eye, could ever be made suitable. But something had to be done and two days later he was writing urgently to the London Missionary Society, pointing out that he found nothing at all that he had been led to believe and nothing at all to his liking. Without reproach, but with firmness, he wrote that he could not start proper medical or surgical practice until he had received from England an adequate supply of medical stores and equipment. He also hinted that some sort of modification or extension to the existing premises would have to be made.

During the six years after James Gilmour's death, the London Missionary Society had made several attempts to find a suitable successor. They had sent out two men, neither of them doctors; but the lawlessness and violence in that area, culminating in some bloody fighting between the Chinese and the Mongols, cut short their activities. The second man, John Parker, had had to leave very recently owing to the collapse of his health. As a legacy to Tom he had left a handful of loyal Chinese Christians, an austere little building rated as a chapel, half a dozen Sunday-school children and the Mongol lease of a plot of land adjoining the small compound which comprised the bungalow and the 'surgery'-cum-waiting room. He had suggested that this plot of land would be useful for Tom to build a proper surgery. But there was no money to spend on building anything.

Western medicine had never been practised by a missionary in this area, and in assigning Tom to his post, it did not seem to have occurred to anyone in London that he would need many things which his predecessors had never required.

A letter from John Parker to the LMS, dated November 19th, 1896, but not received till January 21st, 1897, described what the Cochranes could expect to find on their arrival, but explained that he had not known that Dr Cochrane was married, and enquired if there were any children.

During all his years in Mongolia and China proper, Tom was to find the lack of rapid communication the greatest trial of his life. It took four months at the least, to get a reply to any of his requests, whether it was for money, medicines, or permission to spend money on buildings. The Cochranes had no resources of their own, and the very little money they had had in England, had been spent on medical supplies and instruments.

As it happened, events in Mongolia overtook them so rapidly that towards the end of their three years, their position was like that of a battalion cut off from headquarters; local decisions had to be made, not after a four-month delay, but within days, hours, and sometimes minutes. So poor were their communications and supply lines that in the end it would not be the 'home' mission responsible for them, but the love and loyalty of the Chinese themselves, which would save them from an untimely and horrible end.

There was one part of John Parker's legacy to him that Tom had not counted on. Lien-Yi, the man who had bargained on their behalf with the owners of the terrible junk in which they had crossed the Gulf of Peichihli, had been trained by John Parker as an evangelist. He was however an itinerant preacher who seldom stayed for long in one place.

At noon on this second day at Chaoyang, to the amazement and relief of Tom and Grace, Lien-Yi quietly arrived at their little house, still with the same piece of fur dangling over his left eye, and still with the disposition of helpfulness, whether it was as a bargainer, a preacher, or indeed, a teacher of the Chinese language.

He was received with open arms by both Tom and Grace. It appeared that he had been seriously worried after their departure from Chinese shores, and knowing that many junks had sunk in the ensuing storm, he could not rest till he found passage by another route. He had then ridden with all speed to Chaoyang, and was relieved beyond measure to find his good Scottish friends alive and well and apparently overjoyed to see him. Something about this quiet doctor and his wife had entered into Lien-Yi's spirit, as he explained with much pointing and gesticulation towards his heart. He had felt compelled to follow the Cochranes and offer his services to them in any capacity. Tom accepted him as a man sent from heaven, and indeed thereafter always referred to Lien-Yi as 'Mr Heaven'.

Within an hour, Lien-Yi was to become a member of the household and it was understood that he would stay with the doctor for as long as he was needed, to help him with the language and the organisation of his work and to do his fair share of preaching. Thus a quaint partnership between a Scottish University graduate and a Chinese peasant-evangelist was born. Lien-Yi had a gift of understanding of his own kind, with a degree of compassion which amazed Tom, who had not thought compassion an outstanding Chinese characteristic. He was to learn much from his 'Mr Heaven'.

In the days that followed Mr Heaven's arrival, Tom struggled with the language, using the few idioms he had picked up, greatly encouraged by his Chinese friend. Grace would find the two men, gesticulating and miming, touching various parts of their anatomy, pointing at walls, ceiling, and furniture while Tom practised the correct Chinese word for each object. When patients began to arrive, Lien-Yi would accompany Tom to the dispensary, and act as interpreter, until Tom found that he was soon communicating sufficiently well to ask the right questions and understand the answers. He discovered that the Chinese do not recognise right or left, but describe everything in relation to north, south, east and west. A patient might tell him that he had a bad pain to the east of his stomach. He found that the Chinese understood nothing whatever of their own anatomy or physiology; nothing of the circulation of the blood, the respiratory system, or the function of the heart. After a few days Tom was thanking God that he had brought so few drugs with him, for the Chinese assumed that if they were given even a small supply of drugs to take home, a cure would be greatly accelerated if all the doses were taken at one time.

More grimly, Tom was acutely aware that if he made a serious medical misjudgment, he might lose not only his patient but also his own life. With this in mind, he was careful not to embark on any treatment which he was unable to sustain until the medical equipment and drugs arrived, and to perform no surgery other than very simple procedures. It was not until after Edgar's birth in September that he felt able to deal with many of the various complaints and diseases presented to him. Some of these he would never be able to treat effectively. In this pre-antibiotic era there were no drugs for such diseases as typhoid, typhus, plague, cholera, and diphtheria. Children were often brought to him with the festering scabs of smallpox still on their faces. Rabies was endemic in the large population of half-wild dogs. It was hard to maintain a minimal standard of hygiene even in his own surroundings. Rats were common in every household and of fleas there was no end. Typhus, he knew in particular, was responsible for the death of many missionaries.

It was not till the winter of 1897 that he felt able to put up any in-patients in the two small rooms adjoining his dispensary. In the meantime, he had Grace at his side, who ignoring her own condition as far as she could, helped him unstintingly. She could not bring herself to imitate the language sounds as unselfconsciously as her husband but in her ministrations, particularly to the women and children, she emanated a quiet confidence. The female patients quickly accepted this gentle woman who, obviously pregnant but uncomplaining, excited both their curiosity and sympathy. They fingered her clothing and asked personal and sometimes crude questions which she could not answer.

Within a short time of his arrival, too, Mr Heaven had found Tom his much-needed assistant, Liu-i. He was a farmer's son who had a great desire to become a doctor. This boy, fresh from the fields, found hand-washing before assisting the doctor an unnecessary and unwanted ritual. He liked to keep his nails very long, so that he could scoop up powder or grain easily. With infinite patience, Tom tried to instil into him the principles of hygiene, of medicine, and of surgery. By the time the Cochranes were to flee Mongolia, this boy could perform minor surgery and deal competently with routine medical matters. Later he was to come to Peking and express his ambition to become a qualified doctor.

One of Tom's first in-patients was a man who had travelled a long distance accompanied and cared for by a friend. The patient had been told that western doctors came from faraway, barbarian lands, but that they could nevertheless perform extraordinary cures with their strange instruments. The belief was, however, that if they were treating eyes, they were apt to remove them altogether and pound them into an emulsion and then coat the inside of small black boxes which they used to take pictures of people and things around them. It was wise, therefore, to be cautious about both treatment and the little black boxes. Tom had some difficulty in persuading the man that if he would trust himself to his care and would stay with him for a few days, he thought he might be able to give him back his sight. In a panic the wretched man turned away and tried to grope his way out of the house, but his friend, who had already borne a good deal of inconvenience and had sacrificed money and time to bring him to the 'foreign devil', encouraged him by saying, 'Don't be afraid. You are blind anyway, so he can't do you much harm!' For several days the man stayed, and, lying on an improvised operating table, eventually allowed the doctor to examine his eyes. Tom placated his fear until he was ready to submit himself to the operation. When the bandages were removed and he found he could see, his joy was unbounded and, embracing the man who had given him back his sight, he ran out into the street shouting at the top of his voice, 'I can see! – I can see!'

As the months went by, Tom was to discover from Mr Heaven that the Mission had a network of outlying stations, thanks to

James Gilmour's earlier efforts. Within an area from thirty to one hundred and thirty miles from Chaoyang, there were a number of little brown mud-walled houses which became a first-aid post for local sufferers whenever they could be visited. James Gilmour had never been in a position to offer more than the simplest treatment, but a rich medical field was out there waiting for Dr Tom Cochrane. One outpost lay in an extremely dangerous district, where bandits and soldiers constantly clashed. Travellers had been known to set out for this place and never be seen nor heard of again.

Tom seldom went on these journeys on his own. He was usually accompanied by his assistant Liu-i, or Mr Heaven, or both. Mr Heaven would introduce him to his compatriots as '*womenti taifu*' ('our doctor') in such a proud and affectionate manner that Tom was often welcomed where doors would otherwise have been closed. Sometimes he entered a village where a foreigner had never been seen, and he was curious to note the psychology of the villagers. A man would lean forward and finger the lapel of his coat, and say, 'This is really fine cloth. How much would a suit like that cost?' Then someone would ask him his name, his age, and where he came from. On hearing that he came from England, another would remark, 'Oh, there is a Queen in England, isn't there? What did she say to you about us before you left, and what are you going to tell her when you return?'

While this was going on inside one of the little houses, someone outside would be applying the tip of his tongue to the paper window. Tom would look up and notice a tiny pink spot rapidly growing into the size of a peep-hole and then each of the timid villagers could take a turn at peering into the room.

Tom concluded that what they were trying to find out was why he had left his home across the sea and come to China. Was he there for a political purpose? Was he a trader? or a spy? It never seemed to dawn upon them that he was there for their sakes; that he really cared for them and their happiness and spiritual good. But after watching him for a while, someone would whisper, 'Isn't his hand light, isn't his touch soft?' One day, when he had completed a comparatively simple operation which was marvellous to them, a friend of the patient exclaimed, 'This is what we might expect if Buddha came to earth again!'

He had only to treat one patient with visible success, and the entire village would overwhelm him, crowding and jostling each other to get to the '*taifu*.' It seemed as if there were not a person in the whole place who did not suffer some physical ailment. Festering, evil-smelling diseased or damaged limbs would be thrust at him, and the little room would soon be filled with such a stench that Tom would have to complete his examinations outside in the street. Otherwise the little house might collapse, or he himself might collapse from suffocation in the fetid air. He learned successfully to camouflage his feelings when confronted with these nauseous sights and smells. The Chinese were frequently overwhelmed emotionally at the sight of a foreign doctor cleaning and treating foul cases of disease or injury which their own compatriots would not touch at any price.

At the end of a two-hour or three-hour session, Mr Heaven, by now having a captive and a captivated audience, would begin to preach. He had a ready wit, and so compelling a manner that he would hold his simple peasant audience spellbound. He would carefully adapt his Bible stories into Chinese idiom, portraying Noah, for instance, as a Chinaman with a queue down his back, holding an oiled silk umbrella up against the elements. He always managed to preach and expound the Gospel in a completely Chinese-orientated manner which took into account the differences between the myths and traditions of Buddhism, Taoism, and Confucianism, which in Mongolia had intermingled over the centuries, and to which lamaism – a corrupt form of Buddhism – had been added at the beginning of the 19th century. Mr Heaven could in seconds adroitly unravel any objection to his teaching so that it stood forth as irrefutable truth to its objectors. He had one other priceless gift. He could speak Mongolian to those Mongols who could not understand the Chinese language. Usually, he managed to convey some moral or spiritual point at the end of his sermon so forcefully that his hearers would beg for more.

On one occasion, however, a man who had travelled a hundred miles to see the '*taifu*', and had wormed his way into the crowd, proceeded to tear his clothes off while Mr Heaven was concluding his sermon. For one nasty moment, Tom thought the man was preparing to assault him but it turned out he was suffering from scabies and had an unbearable itch. 'How long have you suffered from this?' Mr Heaven called to the man over the heads of the crowd. 'For two years,' the man yelled back. 'All right, then,' shouted Mr Heaven, 'just suffer for another two minutes till I finish my sermon.' And finish it he did.

In the heat of summer, which in Mongolia was very dry heat,

Tom would make no attempt to go indoors but would set up a trestle table and his equipment on the one little patch of green that each village cultivated in the hot months. This was a free show which the village children enjoyed as much as the visits of the Tibetan magicians or the nomadic tribesmen offering their produce. Those were the only other strangers they ever saw.

After the long, hard winter of 1897-8, when Tom had spent all day and every day of the week except Sunday in his cramped dimly-lit dispensary in Chaoyang, he found these 'trips' were almost equal to a holiday in therapeutic value, especially when accompanied by Mr Heaven with his irrepressible sense of humour. He insisted that the villagers would understand Tom better if he dressed like a Chinese and wore a queue. 'Besides, *Taifu*,' he said solemnly, 'you are too handsome to be a foreigner. God meant you to be a Chinese!' 'And another thing,' he added, 'they will *smile* more if they think you are one of them

On their next trip, as a result of Mr Heaven's advice, two Chinamen immaculate in dress and queue rode out of Chaoyang.

As Lien-Yi had foreseen, the metamorphosis from 'foreign devil' in western clothes into kindly Chinese doctor with a queue broke down any residual distrust which the villagers had. This sometimes led to informal scenes of downright hilarity, as when on one occasion, after treating about fifty patients, Tom was tired and sitting on a backless bench, leaned back against a stone wall. A small boy skilfully managed to kick away one of the legs of the bench, trapping the doctor in an undignified position between the wall and the bench. At that precise moment, an old man sitting nearby, who had adopted the Chinese habit of slipping his right hand up the wide left sleeve of his tunic, and his left hand up the wide right sleeve, nodded off, to the delight of the younger people. He fell forward on to his nose, and lay stiffly, still asleep with folded arms, like a fallen idol. Another small boy, who had borrowed the family god (a live hedgehog) from its tiny mud shrine by the side of a nearby house, promptly seized the opportunity to apply the hedgehog to the old man's bare leg, where his cotton sock had descended round his ankle.

On a refuse heap, the better to see an unusual sight, stood a bevy of village beauties. In their red trousers, and balancing themselves on their tiny hoof-like feet, they made a bright patch on an otherwise drab background. On this occasion, Mr Heaven extended his peroration to such time as the doctor was rescued, the old man awakened and restored to a sitting position, and the hedgehog returned to its shrine. He finished in fact, amongst some mirth on the part of his listeners, with a homily concerning the 'kitchen god', one of his favourite themes.

Of all his work in Mongolia, and despite the danger which attended every foray into the territory north of Chaoyang (he was chased more than once by bandits into the nearest shuttered and gated inn, which alone saved him), Tom enjoyed most these visits to the poor peasants of mixed Mongol and Chinese origins, who so deeply came to appreciate his services and his friendship. Here he met no opposition, no hostility or criticism of anything he did. The need for medical help was infinite and he felt as he moved amongst them that he was at last fulfilling a longed-for role. He had opted to become a doctor rather than a minister because he knew he could express his love and concern more through the work of his hands and his brain than through the words of his lips.

Besides, with Mr Heaven at his side, who needed him to do any preaching? He was satisfied with their partnership, and thanked his God every day that the path had been made so plain for him. His love for these people and his friendship with them grew.

If only London did not take so long to answer his letters and supply his needs! Perhaps, if he managed to last the ten-year term to which he was committed in this place, communications might with time improve, and then his work could be speeded up.

Time, however, was not on Tom's side in this or any other matter. Just as he was thanking God that one part of his work, at least, seemed full of promise, something happened which changed the direction of his life.

Towards the end of that summer, a huge influx of robbers and bandits – nobody knew where they came from – poured into the Chaoyang district, surrounding the City and even penetrating into it. They plundered, pillaged, and tortured as they went. Cartloads of women and children fled, some from the town to the country, others from the country to the town. Carts which normally would carry only two or three people had nearly a dozen women and children crammed into them. There was chaos everywhere.

The Cochranes had finally decided to leave, but suddenly there were no carts to be had, and simultaneously they heard that the gates of the city had been closed and barricaded as the panic reached its climax.

And then, before they knew what was happening, the Mission

Compound was seized. Bandits rode into their compound, and were at their door, demanding the sum of 1,000 taels of silver, or they would all be put to torture. A terrified Grace, with a screaming baby in her arms, stood by Tom's side as he tried to explain to the bandit leader that he had not got 1,000 taels. Lien-Yi bravely expostulated with the robbers, explaining that the '*taifu*' was poor and all he did, he did for the poor, without reward. Slightly, but only slightly, mollified, the bandits eventually rode off, declaring that if the money was not forthcoming within two days' time, they would return and carry out their threats.

Shocked and trembling, Tom and Grace re-entered the house, barricading all the doors and windows, but with the knowledge that nothing they could do would keep the bandits out if they chose to return. Grace would not put the baby down, but held him closely all through the night. Together with Lien-Yi and their one Chinese servant who was also a Christian, they pleaded with their Father in heaven to deliver them out of danger and tell them what to do. Tom slowly recited the 91st Psalm, which in later life he said had always been a source of strength in moments of danger. But they did not go to bed for fear they might be besieged while asleep.

By the following evening, they heard that the authorities had sent in a sufficient number of soldiery to clear the bandits out of the city and out of the neighbourhood. But as autumn approached, there were no more trips into the countryside for Tom. He had many other preoccupations and just before Christmas of 1898 Grace discovered that she was pregnant again.

4

Punishments and Prisoners

It was late Spring of 1899 before Tom could assess his own progress objectively. His morning time of prayer became the place of even greater self examination and commitment as he began to plan to create a six-bedded 'hospital' from a small building nearby, to resume his village work with Lien-Yi in the warmer weather, and to open a new station in the dangerous district of Yang Shan. He was also concerned about his own health. At the end of the long, bitterly cold winter he felt a terrible inertia weighing him down. He was perpetually covered in flea-bites and frequently suffered stomach cramps when working in his dispensary or visiting. Neither the climate nor the Chinese diet suited him. *'I don't know whether or not this dejection is occasioned by the climate or loneliness,'* he wrote, *'but it is hard to bear and cuts the nerve of effort. Oh my God, forsake me not.'* The claustrophobic effect of the hills around Chaoyang was one cause of his depression; another was that he missed the companionship of medical colleagues from the old days in Glasgow.

He had arrived with practically no knowledge of Mongolia's various religious cultures. He had found three main religions, Confucianism, Buddhism, and Taoism. Of these he considered Confucianism the purest, Buddhism (infected by the blight of lamaism) the most corrupt and Taoism the most superstitious and fearful.

He summarised his impressions of Mongolia in diaries, letters and reports, formal or informal, to friends and well-wishers at home. He could now describe who were his friends and who were his enemies.

He started with the enemies: Lamas and bandits. Tom was not sure who were the more responsible for the miseries of Mongolia. Bandits were the most obvious menace to life and property, but bandits were outside the law of the land, and were enemies to everybody. They were materially but not spiritually dangerous. But the lamas! . . . They were a curse on the soul of the people.

Tom now knew that the lama temple and its priests exerted a most powerful and exacting influence over the whole country. The lamas belonged to the 'Yellow Hat' sect of Tibetan Buddhists, a sect riddled with homosexuality. They had been thrown out of Tibet at the beginning of the 19th century, and had spread across Mongolia, establishing a lamasery in every district, which in turn became the nucleus of a Mongolian township. Priests owned half the cattle and the land and lamas represented twenty per cent of the population. They imposed vicious taxes on the bulk of the peasants' produce and exploited the pilgrims who visited the Chaoyang lamasery as they passed on their way to the sacred mountains of Wutaim in Northern China. The sect was flagrant in sexual deviations and since the lamas constituted sixty per cent of the male Mongol population, the country was said to be in danger of under population.

Tom had revisited the temple several times when called out to attend a sick lama. He had tried to establish an understanding with the lamas and talk with them on spiritual matters; but he felt that his words were wafted away in the whirr of prayer wheels and the murmur of the mantra. He always left the temple weighed down with a sense of brooding darkness and evil. He was not surprised when he discovered that the 'Yellow Hats' practiced demon-worship.

Eventually he had come face to face with the Head Lama. Surprisingly, this man came to his dispensary as a patient, albeit condescendingly. He described certain symptoms for which Tom gave him medicine. He returned a month later and smilingly described his new condition. Tom explained that this was to be expected as a consequence of the remedies he had prescribed for him. 'But,' said the Head Lama with obvious relish, 'I did not take your medicine!' Immediately Tom realised that the man must have suborned his assistant to learn what results would follow the treatment and that his sole intention now was to humiliate him. When the Head Lama took his hand in his own and gave him a veiled but unflattering description of his character, Tom was convinced of this. In the following weeks he came to realise that this powerful individual would not hesitate to stop his missionary work, even if it meant killing him. Other powerful interests were ranged against him, particularly opium-den owners whose livelihood he threatened. He was warned of one who was going around with a loaded gun seeking an opportunity to kill him.

Tom laid down his pen and pondered on what he had already written. As he paused, he considered how on earth he could possibly convey to the Mission and to his Scottish friends and supporters, the monumental scope of his work. In despairing mood he remembered one section of the Mongolian people whose sufferings he had been totally unable to relieve. These were the prisoners confined in the jail adjacent to the Yamen building, savagely and all too often condemned to death for crimes they had not committed, and from which there was no appeal.

Strictly from the LMS point of view, they did not come within the terms of his commission. But, he wondered, did the people of Great Britain, the Christians who had selected him to be their representative of Christ, have the faintest idea of what life was like in a pagan country?

As Tom considered the nature and the needs of this dark and God-forsaken country, he mused on the corruption which beset high places both in the civil law and administration and in the Lamaist religious sphere. The 'Yellow Hats' imposed iniquitous taxation of people already so poor that they were sometimes starving. When they could not pay, the Yamen stepped in and had them arrested as debtors, punished with prison sentences and frequently executed without mercy.

Thus, lamas were enemies; opium den owners were enemies. The position of 'the authorities' towards him was uncertain. But he was appalled by their callous treatment of their own people.

Unless and until the law could be reformed and the blight of lamaism swept out of the country, there was no way in which any foreign Christian missionary, be he doctor or evangelist, could effectively bring hope or healing to these victims of a cruel and vicious religio-legal system.

He decided that he must spare the Missionary Society and his own friends and family nothing and that he would write of these things exactly as he found them. He then wrote this fearful indictment –

'From these vile prisons, about every other week – in troublous times every few days, men are led out to suffer the death penalty. I have seen these poor mortals leave their prison house, dirty, ragged and wretched, and too dazed seemingly to realise their fast approaching doom. They are huddled together in an open cart and conveyed through the crowded streets to a sandy depression outside the town, and here, in presence of a multitude of spectators who stand on the high ground, they kneel in a row. The assistant grasps the pigtail and pulls upon it to stretch their neck and then the executioner with his sword does what the Chinese think is a dreadful thing – sends them into the next world without a head. The bodies are often not buried and the dogs and the pigs devour them. I have gone through the execution grounds when the sights were past description. Sometimes the native doctors buy certain parts of the remains. The head is frequently made into a decoction to make men brave. Certain bones too are powdered and administered for the control of haemorrhage.' (A marginal and almost indecipherable note says, '*Flesh . . . per lb, sold, dear.*')

After such visits to the execution grounds Grace would find him, sitting hunched up on the side of their bed, his face covered by his hands and trembling till the bed shook. 'You've not to take it so much into yourself, Tom' she said on one occasion. 'It isn't your doing. They're just evil and wicked men.'

Tom was not sure to which men she was referring and wished that he could dismiss the subject so forthrightly. But he could not forget that Jesus had said, 'The spirit of the Lord is upon me, because he hath anointed me to preach the gospel to the poor; he hath sent me to heal the broken-hearted, to preach deliverance to the captives and recovery of sight to the blind, to set at liberty them that are bruised.'

This was also his own commission. Which of these five injunctions had he been able to fulfil? He had, in the last year, given recovery of sight to many blind people, an act considered a miracle by the Mongols; he had done his best to heal the broken-hearted by reviving their spirits and their health; he and Mr Heaven together were continually preaching the gospel to the poor. But . . . 'preach deliverance to the captives?' – 'set at liberty them that are bruised?' If this was meant literally, he had dismally failed. He had never been allowed into the town jail, nor to minister at an execution, and he did not know where he stood with the Mandarins or magistrates. So far he himself had not been on any occasion involved in legal proceedings. He knew, however, that the stipend of magistrates was so inadequate that they were forced to live on bribes in order to keep up the large retinue expected of them. Even the jailers could be bribed to suffocate a man's enemy in jail if offered sufficient money. Certainly he could not use that method to gain admittance, even if he had had the means. That was not the way of Jesus. He tried to think of some precedent for his condition, but could think of none. He prayed that he might be given more insight into this problem and turned his attention to all the other kinds and conditions of men he had been sent to.

The appeal of James Gilmour's ministry had been mainly to a particular section of the Mongolian population, the nomadic tribesmen of the northern plains, whose constant movement from place to place had helped maintain their independence and relative freedom from the oppression of the lamas. Mongols had once ruled the mightiest Empire on earth, and its people had been warlike and dominating. Their nomadic descendents still had a hardness and a toughness not found in the urban Mongols or the Chinese. He remembered a conversation he had had with a very old Mongol who had visited him at his dispensary soon after his and Grace's arrival in Chaoyang.

At certain seasons, the nomads rode into town for markets, fairs and festivals. They came in hordes, riding their fast little ponies into town, carrying with them anything they could sell or barter. Mostly they brought dairy products and lamb which they would gladly exchange for grain or oats, or for the copper and brass kettles which were essential to their way of life with its continual tea-drinking. They were good customers to the urban inhabitants who did not, however, greatly admire their greasy, shaggy locks and their dirty sheepskin coats. The Chinese used to say that the nomads 'took only one bath a year, if they needed it.'

On one of these outings, an old nomad had left his pony in the market place and had wandered into Tom's dispensary, bowed low with great dignity, and explained that he wanted to meet the man who had succeeded his great friend James Gilmour. There was an air of curiosity about the old man. Tom was not quite sure whether he had come as a spy to report back to the others, or whether he might be a genuine 'enquirer' after the truth, or perhaps just wanted some medicine. He was soon to be enlightened.

This ancient was sparse of hair, wrinkled and yellow of complexion, his skin hanging on him like a folded garment. His dark eyes, hooded and sunken, darted from side to side with the unmistakeable gleam of Mongolian slyness. Tom felt he was in the presence of a man as old as time itself, and as earthy as the earth itself. He felt that here was one who would not take his counsels easily but would pit his own logic and experience against all comers.

The old man came straight to the point. He and his fellow nomads had liked and admired James Gilmour. Had they not shared their tents with him, eaten their food with him, taught him the secrets of desert life, and encouraged him to ride the fast ponies with the short stirrups which the foreigner usually hated, and to care for his camels in the approved Mongol fashion? Of course James had in turn given them simple medicines and had been a good friend to them, but he had known better than to preach any new thing to them, because as good Confucians they already knew all that was necessary for this life. How otherwise could they survive the hazards of their climate? Sometimes they could not move out of their tents for weeks at a time, because they were buried under tons of sand which bore down on them in a sandstorm; and sometimes they were trapped in their tents by icy cold which froze everything rock hard. Sometimes it was too hot for the ponies to move, and in a drought the cattle could die of thirst. They themselves being part of the earth, these natural events were not disasters to them. They were neither afraid of life nor death. So why had the good doctor come to replace their friend, who had realised the superiority of Confucius over all other authorities? Their ancestors had followed his teaching for centuries. Who was this Jesus whom he had been told the doctor had come to declare and why should they be invited to follow him when they already had their own Confucius? If he were so important, then why had he not been born a Mongol, or at least a Chinese?

The old man paused for breath and Tom realised that he had already gone over this ground many times before and did not really want a reply to his rhetorical questions. He was obviously on the attack and Tom decided to lead him on and let him have his full say.

'And besides,' the old man went on, brushing aside Tom's silence as though it had been an objection, 'you know very well, *Taifu*, that a good Confucian does not have any sins, so he does not need a saviour. You insult a Confucian if you tell him he is a sinner.'

Tom was glad he had said nothing.

'You see,' the old man said, as he warmed to his subject even further, 'it is not right for a foreigner to suggest such things to a Mongol. You may say it to a Chinese, who is very much in need of such talk, because he wrongly considers himself superior to his Mongol neighbours. But if you stay here long enough you will find out for yourself that what I say is true. The Chinese do not tell lies as competently as we do; if they thieve, they do it badly and then get caught. So, as everybody knows, if you cannot get the better of your neighbour, you are inferior and not so good.'

Tom could not help smiling at this ingenious piece of logic. He decided it was time to turn the talk to more spiritual levels. But again, as if he had read his thoughts, the old man raced ahead, determined to forestall any disagreement.

'You must know, *Taifu*,' he said, 'we are the oldest people on earth. Although we wander about, we belong to the earth and it belongs to us. So what is there to tell us that we do not already know? When we die, our bodies go back to the earth, and that is all there is to it. I believe,' he added shrewdly, 'that is also what you say in words when you bury your dead, although you do not worship your ancestors as these foolish Chinese do. We could not possibly care for the graves of our fathers because we move about so much that we would never find them again in the sand. Besides, why should we have to pay for food for our ancestors in the spirit world when we do not believe in a spirit world?'

He paused, literally, for breath. Tom glanced at Mr Heaven who had been quietly standing a little to one side, interpreting the conversation. Mr Heaven gave a gentle shake of the head in response to Tom's look of enquiry, but slid one hand meaningly up the sleeve of his tunic. Tom remembered the bartering sessions at Peichihli for the hire of the junk and realised he was being given the signal to come to terms with the old man. In a flash he recognised that this ancient Mongol had not come just to air his views, or even out of simple curiosity. There was something he wanted from Tom but was too proud to ask for. Tom abandoned all thought of preaching to him, or even replying to his statements, but with Mr Heaven's aid he tactfully brought the conversation round to the subject of the old man's health and any possible needs he might have. After several denials of the idea that he could possibly be in need of anything, the old man left, triumphantly clutching a package of pills, after bowing very low once more to Tom, assuring him that any time he would like to visit him in the desert, he would gladly share his tent with him – if Tom could find it. 'But,' he said in final parting, 'if you come, *Taifu*, do not come on a camel, because I have three camels and I am afraid they would not welcome a strange camel in their midst.'

Tom went to the door and gazed after him disconsolately, but on return he saw that Mr Heaven was smiling at him. '*Taifu*,' he said, 'do not be upset. The good James heard these words many times, even after he had lived with them for years and suffered their hardships with them. In any case, the nomads are all Buddhists, not Confucians, and he was just trying to confuse you. The nomads love to see their sons become lamas; it is their highest ambition. The old man had one, I believe, but he died. I tell you, the nomads do not want to change.'

It was not so, however, with the poorer section of the Mongol population who had drifted away from their clansmen of the northern plains and in one or two generations had become urbanised. They lived in the poorest parts of the city, in houses which were often roofless and exposed to the extreme cold in winter and to the silting up of sand in their houses which occurred at every sandstorm, at any time of the year. They had intermarried with the Chinese, their traditional enemies, and it was sometimes difficult to decide of which stock they came. Tom had never in his life seen such poverty and relentless hardship endured by any people. In most of the homes that he visited, the whole family lived in one room, the single fire heating the *kang* on which they crowded together by day and on which they slept side by side at night. They used manure for fuel, picked up in the streets and dried. Meals consisted of porridge made from millet, or steamed bread made from a dark sorghum flour normally used for animals. If there was any relief from their monotonous diet, it was a flavouring of pickled turnip tops fermented in large jars, and abominably acrid.

Like the villagers of the countryside, these poorest of the poor in Mongolian society accepted Tom's helping hand with gratitude. They could pay nothing and they could repay nothing. As Tom watched their fortitude, he could find no fault in them. 'We are of those who are destined to feed on bitterness', they said of themselves; but they showed no bitterness. Occasionally, he would find a man or a woman lying on the *kang* inhaling opium fumes from a pipe, but he could never find it in his heart to reprove them. When they referred to the drug as 'the foreign smoke', the very words sent a stab of shame through Tom, because of his own nation's responsibility in forcing the sale of this vile narcotic on to a helpless people. He turned the reproach upon himself and could only promise help and encouragement to any who would agree to be treated. Frequently the opium addict would express hatred for it and accepted Tom's help.

Regretfully, Tom decided that he was only totally accepted by these poor, simple people and by the peasants. They alone appreciated the message brought to them by Mr Heaven. Ninety per cent of them were illiterate and unused to any mental effort. To teach one person to read the simplest Chinese ideographs would take a year of one man's sustained effort, and to teach him the fundamentals of the faith an infinitely longer time. Tom had to be content in the midst of all his other work, to serve them physically and relieve some of their sufferings.

Of his popularity as a doctor there could be no doubt. There were days when he saw as many as one hundred patients. He had written frantically to the London Missionary Society pointing out the deficiencies of his medical accommodation. '*The women who come to the dispensary sit in the yard at our back door, and not infrequently smallpox and other infectious cases or their friends . . . make their way into our sitting room to ask for medicines.*' He implored the Mission to send him funds to build a separate waiting room for the women. Against Chinese custom and his own preference, male and female patients herded together in the one tiny waiting room. When it was full, the remainder had to sit outside in the small compound at the mercy of the elements; some had developed frostbite and then needed double attention when they were at last seen.

Many patients came long distances, often having sacrificed as much as three months' pay in order to make the journey and pay the expenses of bearers or friends accompanying them. By the time they arrived, they had frequently run out of food and money, expecting to be admitted to a free hospital for an unlimited time. Too often it was clear they had come too late and sadly Tom had to say there was nothing he could do. Some arrived, as one woman did nursing her baby, in a basket carried by her menfolk who had roped the basket over their shoulders. Others came on improvised stretchers, consisting of one leaf of a door. Many he saw once and never saw again.

Most of his dispensary patients were ethnically Han Chinese. James Gilmour had found how difficult it was for both Mongols and Chinese to become Christians, but for different reasons. For the nomads it would have entailed severance from their tribe, family and cattle, which was unthinkable and James had never urged it on them.

The difficulties for the Chinese were due to their own religious beliefs. The religious beliefs of the Han Chinese in and around the Chaoyang district, just north of the Great Wall, were a hopeless mixture of the three main religions. The strangling influence of ancestor worship was particularly strong. Unlike the Confucians, Buddhists and Taoists believed in a spirit world and a life hereafter. Taoism in particular had introduced a fantastic array of gods or spirits which lived behind every material object, from cooking pots to trees. They could wreak vengeance on mortals if they were offended or neglected and were devoid of moral sense. In addition to this pantheon, a home had to have its own tangible idol with its shrine which must be tended at all times. Sometimes the 'god' was a living creature, like the hedgehog who was a 'kitchen god'. The whole of life was imbued with the necessity of placating these deities. The terrors of life did not end at the grave, however, for the work of placating the guardians of the underworld passed on to the children when their parents died. Tom knew of one case where an elderly father had literally prostrated himself at the feet of his son, entreating him to renounce this foreign 'Way'. Otherwise he feared he himself would have to wander starved and naked in the unseen world.

When a Chinaman died, the following funeral rituals had to be performed: a paper horse and cart had to be burnt to accompany the spirit of the departed; a cake with plenty of hairs in it had to be placed in the coffin, pieces of which the wanderer would throw to the dogs if they disputed his entrance into the spirit world, trusting that the hairs would choke them. Corn had to be thrown to the hens and paper money burnt for his use. Idols and ancestors must be worshipped indefinitely. Food must be placed regularly on the grave. '*It is not to be wondered at,*' wrote Tom in a report, '*if sons are threatened with torture and death unless they recant.*'

On the other side of the spiritual ledger, Tom found some hope and reason for optimism in balancing the difficulties against the rewards. As he sat one morning in his early quiet hour, he thought he saw daylight in his decision to make charges for medical work for those who could afford it. In time his little hospital would become self-supporting and then it could be enlarged. If he could train more men like Liu-i then it might become a real Chinese hospital indigenous to the country in character and style. Perhaps even the lamas . . . His dream was interrupted by a knock on the door. Grace rarely disturbed him in his early morning 'hour', but she stood now in the doorway, looking worried but determined. She had come to remind Tom that her monthly pre-natal examination was overdue. By her reckoning she thought she was nearly seven months pregnant.

Apologising for his oversight, Tom began his examination in his usual methodical manner. Halfway through he put down his stethoscope. Then he picked it up again and carefully went all through the routine again. Grace looked at him apprehensively. 'Is everything all right, Tom?' she asked. 'I've just been wondering . . .'

'Grace,' he said, 'I've just heard two foetal hearts. I can feel two sets of skeletal spine. My dear, you are going to have twins!'

5

Escape from Chaoyang

The twins were born on August 11th, 1899, at the North China seaside resort of Peitaiho. Tom was assisted by an English woman doctor, Doctor Saville, who on hearing of the Cochranes' dilemma in Chaoyang had immediately offered more suitable accommodation and medical facilities, plus her own services. The fact that Grace was expecting twins and that she was not in the best of health made the offer irresistible, though Tom was reluctant to defer his plans and expectations of expanding his work at that point. As it was, the twins were nearly a month premature, and the journey from Chaoyang to Peitaiho was excruciatingly uncomfortable. The Cochranes arrived only just in time.

Robert and Thomas were fraternal, not identical, twins. They were as unlike Edgar as it was possible to be. They lacked his energy and robustness. They had their father's fine features but resembled their mother not at all. They had fair, downy hair, and their eyes, far from turning near-black as Edgar's had, stayed permanently blue. This feature was going to prove a source of great danger to them later. They were fragile babies and needed special care.

The Cochranes' stay in this favourite watering place for Europeans on holiday in Northern China was an undisguised blessing. The comparatively bracing atmosphere by the sea, after the dead, shut-in air of Chaoyang revived Tom's drooping spirits. The kindness and care of Doctor Saville, the rest, and the experience of being looked after by another British woman in civilised and comfortable surroundings soon put Grace back on her feet. It was the babies' delicacy of health which caused the Cochranes to prolong their stay well into October. They both had respiratory and stomach troubles, and their fragility was in sharp contrast to Edgar's boisterous health. Edgar at two years old was a lively child and he was developing a healthy independence and a daring spirit – too daring, his mother thought – when she remembered the risks and dangers of Chaoyang. If Tom had told her that they would not be returning there but that their next assignment was to be on the moon, Grace would gladly have agreed. She dreaded going back to Mongolia. In fact, all her subliminal fears had been realised in their absence. Because of prolonged drought, many more people were hungry, and brigandage was rife once more, as they found when they arrived home.

Although their Christian friends welcomed the Cochrane family back, and the twins were greatly admired, Tom sensed new and sinister elements in the atmosphere of the already troubled country. There was a sharper note in the voices of the anti-foreign troublemakers in Chaoyang. Tom heard murmurings and whispered invectives behind his back as he went about the city. One day, as Grace was showing off the twins to a crowd of patients who were commenting on their blue eyes, someone at the back of the crowd quietly repeated a chant that was later to become a national slogan and a roar of hatred:

Yen fa lan,
Ti fa Kan

which meant:

'Their eyes are blue
Hence earth lacks dew'

This ditty was increasingly used in the future to stir up Mongolian fear and hatred for the 'hairy barbarians' of the West whom they accused of using magical powers to cause continuous drought and the failure of that year's harvest.

There were changes, too, in the Cochrane household. They had been joined by the Rev and Mrs Liddell, sent out by the London Missionary Society who realised the doctor's medical work was so demanding that he needed help with his preaching. Tom was thus relieved of some of the pressures of Sundays. Mr Liddell took over services in the little chapel and also taught the weekday Bible classes to which a smattering of literate Chinese came. He also began to teach the illiterate with Chinese ideographs and prepared them with a small catechism for baptism and entry into the Church.

The trickle of converts, however, now began to dry up completely and just as Tom was again preparing to make the small hospital self-supporting by introducing fees for those who could afford them, suddenly there was a row of empty beds and nobody seemed to require one. At last he had the much longed-for 'ladies only' waiting room, but suddenly there were no patients to use it. Some of the few patients who now attended the dispensary showed evidence of torture – hacked by some kind of metal weapon or horribly burned – for the bandits' activities were now in full spate. The little bungalow seemed grossly overcrowded with the twins and the Liddells added to the household. The Liddells had no children as yet (their son, Eric, who was the subject of the film *Chariots of Fire* was born in 1901 and went to school in England with all three Cochrane brothers) and Grace was the only person whose time was fully occupied. She was by now so preoccupied with the care of her three children that she seemed hardly aware of what was going on outside the four walls of the house. If she was aware of the danger, she saw no sense in brooding over it, but quietly kept the household going in an orderly fashion. Many years later, her son, Dr Robert Cochrane, world-famous leprologist, testified to his mother's fortitude: '*it was she who, in days of danger and peril – peril through climate, peril through disease, peril from bandits – shared my father's life. It was she who, in later years, during the intervals when the head of the family was away, kept the lamp of faith burning bright at the family altar. There was incident after incident which could have ended in death or worse, but for the good hand of the Lord upon the family.*'

At times Tom had to leave Chaoyang and travel by a rough mountain road to fetch lump silver which was the local currency. This was chopped up, weighed and exchanged for copper 'cash'. Fifty pence (at 1983's value) of this was a load nobody could carry very far. A 'cash' was a round copper coin with a square hole in the centre. Often the coin was so thin that little more than the hole existed. Tom used to thread these coins on to a thin rope around his waist beneath the Chinese clothes he now always wore when he was crossing the country. Two 'cash' paid for a night's stay at a Chinese inn. Tom considered this expensive, especially at the inn he had to use on the mountain road on a journey he undertook at the beginning of February, 1900. This inn was more dilapidated and dirty than usual, and he felt inclined to sleep outside in the cart. But it was bitterly cold and he decided to go inside. He asked his host to light the *kang*. He took off his boots and sat like a trussed fowl while the innkeeper thrust lighted kaoling stalks into the opening of the flue immediately below him. The acrid smoke made tears roll down his cheeks, but while waiting for the evening meal, he overheard a chilling conversation in the adjoining room. Two men were discussing the current troubles, and from their tone Tom suspected they were themselves bandits.

The first man remarked that there was a 'foreign devil' in the inn. The other replied that yes, he had seen him and he was different from others he had seen. This one did not have blue eyes, but black like his own, and he had black hair. He also had a fine nose and was as good-looking as a Chinese and could easily pass for one. The first voice replied that foreigners always spoke Chinese with an accent, their gestures were different and above all they *smelt* different. They had a milky smell which they themselves disliked and that was why they bathed themselves so often. The voice added, after a pause, that it did not matter, as the Chinese would soon be rid of them all.

His friend retorted that that was a good thing as otherwise the Westerners would slice the country up like a melon. He had heard a rumour that there had been trouble in Shanghai and that the German Emperor had landed there. Then the King of France had arrived, then the King of England, and one could be sure in these circumstances that the Tsar of Russia was not far away. The Emperor of China, he said, had sent an envoy, exchanged gifts, and talked peace, for he well knew that soon the Chinese would sweep all these barbarians into the sea.

'Good!' was the final response. 'What if we begin with the one in the next room?'

Tom chewed on his indigestible dough strings, swallowed a cup of anaemic looking tea and returned to his cart as swiftly as he could. He drove on for a few miles, then selected as sheltered a spot as he could find and spent the rest of the night there, in the cart. He reflected grimly that his six-month old twins were at risk of death on account of their blue eyes, which neither of their parents had. He himself had been warned.

By the time he returned from this trip, fewer and fewer patients were coming to the dispensary, but Tom was still called out to cases of emergency. He was by now fully aware of the rumours circulating which attributed sinister motives to his medical work. He ignored all this and carried on with whatever work came to hand. One of the last cases he attended was of a macabre nature which had its humorous side. This was a case of a man who saved his life by cutting his throat! The Chinese razor has a short blade, and the would-be suicide cannot apply it as he would a longer blade. In this case the short, sawing motion of the stumpy blade merely notched the windpipe and left the large vessels of the neck uninjured. This man was in a towering rage and had wanted to be revenged on his enemies by making an exit from this world which would involve them in endless trouble. When his first effort failed, he was so disappointed to find himself still alive that he jumped head first down a well. There was so little water in the well that though it covered his nose and mouth it did not reach his neck, and he continued to breathe through the hole he had made. He was pulled out by the heels, and was so infuriated by his failure that he called in the foreign doctor to stitch up the hole till he could decide what further action to take.

As Tom emerged from the man's house having performed this service, he pondered on the swing from the sublime to the ridiculous. He had come out to Mongolia with the avowed hope that the whole country should be evangelised and changed through his medical ministry. He was now reduced to putting stitches in one would-be suicide's self-inflicted wound. His assistant, Liu-i, could have done this equally well. As he considered this, a mass of confused thinking rose to the surface of his mind. A few days earlier had written in his diary, '*My Father, I have several difficulties and one is to know what thoughts are legitimate and what are not . . .*' He had been afraid to face what he now acknowledged to himself, that for a missionary to spend a lifetime in giving such personal service as he was doing was an extravagant use of his capacities. Surely the alternative was to surround himself with Christian students, like Liu-i, who could practice what they learned from him amongst their own people. Just as Mr Heaven was able to reach his Mongolian hearers in their own idiom far better than Tom could, so men like Liu-i would not be hindered by the prejudices and superstitions of their own people which would always hinder Tom. He returned home determined to use his remaining time making Liu-i as competent as it was humanly possible. For the first time, Tom accepted that he might have to leave his post, and that his days were probably numbered.

For some time now maps had been circulating around the inns and other public places in Mongolia. A Russian bear was portrayed lying upon Manchuria and stretching its paws southwards. A British lion was squatting over the valley of the Yangtze river. A Gallic cock was dominating the territory adjoining Indo-China, and the province of Shantung was encircled by a German sausage! China, which for over two thousand years had considered herself the hub of the universe, and the centre of all civilisation and art, now found herself in a beleaguered position by the Western powers. To the Chinese all Europeans were 'hairy barbarians', totally inferior to themselves in every way. But over the 19th century there had been more and more encroachment upon Chinese territory by the Western powers and Russia, backed up by gunboat diplomacy especially on the part of Britain. China had been forced to make enormous trading concessions to foreign powers and pay huge indemnities after there had been trouble. Bitterness over the so-called 'Opium War' of 1840, above all, had meant that 'ivory tower' isolationism on the part of China had dissolved into active and virulent hatred of all the Western powers. Feeling was fanned by the various anti-foreign secret societies, outstandingly by the Society of Harmonious Fists, otherwise known as the 'Boxers' on account of their habit of shadow boxing while practicing the martial arts. The 'Boxers' were obsessed with fanatical zeal to drive out or kill all foreigners and had formed armed bands of terrorists who roamed the country. They were also out to destroy all Christians, and they hated and despised Chinese Christians even more than foreign ones. Their mad hatred had also given them the conviction that they were physically invulnerable and that no foreign arms, including bullets, could penetrate their flesh. They themselves did all their killing or torture with knives or swords. Their boldness made an appeal to the Manchu Empress-Dowager, Tzu-hsi, and exacerbated her own xenophobia.

There were some at the Imperial Court in Peking who urged an accommodation with the Western powers and were outspoken in condemnation of the Boxer movement, urging the Empress-Dowager to disband them. In the end, however, three leading exponents of this view were executed in quick succession on the Empress-Dowager's orders, and thereafter she assimilated the Boxers, ragged, ruffianly and undisciplined as they were, into the Imperial Army. The new war cry, initiated by the Empress-

Dowager herself was, '*Kill the foreigners, kill the foreigners, kill them before breakfast!*'

From that moment, all Chinese Christians and every Westerner in North China were in deadly peril. The aim of the Government, now aided by the Boxer forces, was to wipe out completely every trace of the Christian religion and every Christian in the whole of China. Thousands of missionaries, both Catholic and Protestant, were killed in the most cruel and ferocious manner with their children, including babies in arms. One of the Boxers' favourite ways of despatching their victims was to lead them into the shed which housed the village straw cutter, a very powerful instrument consisting of a long sharp knife mounted on a board, with a contrivance which slammed it down on to the human body lengthwise, cutting it into two as neatly as it did the bales of straw when they were being prepared for stacking. This was often preceded by days of pursuit and torture of all kinds before the long knife finally had its way. Many Chinese were martyred along with their Western brothers and sisters, and many displayed the utmost courage and determination. Many of them cried out forgiveness to their murderers as they were despatched. Grim stories began to filter into Chaoyang, with details too horrifying for Tom to describe to his wife. It was useless to appeal to the *yamen* – the residence of a mandarin – for any protection, for they heard that missionaries in some districts who had done this had been executed as criminals, and others who had tried to reach the presumed safety of a *yamen* had been overtaken and murdered by the roadside.

It was equally useless to expect any protection or advice from the Consul, or from London Mission Headquarters. In the end, they barred and shuttered the doors and windows of the little bungalow and decided that the question was now one of personal decision. After two hours' talk it was agreed that Grace, the children, and Mrs Liddell, would attempt to escape to the railhead some sixty miles away, in carts. Mr Liddell would escort them to safety, and then return if possible to Chaoyang. Tom felt that it was his absolute duty to remain behind with his Christian friends. All of them were secretly loath to believe that this would prove more than a temporary escape and that when it was all over life would return to whatever normality Chaoyang had ever possessed.

The problem now, as it had been in the earlier incident when they had tried to flee the Mission from the bandits, was that of finding carts. One man well-known to the doctor promised to try and get one, but his old mother forbade him to risk it. Finally, through another friendly Chinese, a cart was obtained, the passengers packed what hand luggage they could, and crowded into it. In the darkness of the night they left their barricaded home and set off on their dangerous journey in the care of a Christian carter.

Tom was left alone, and as he re-entered the bungalow and sat down in the living room, he experienced an anguish of soul that for the rest of his life he could always recall but never describe. All that was precious to him in this world, his wife, his three sons, and his friends were out on those dark roads with menace and danger at every turn. If they encountered Boxers, what hope had they of escape? As reaction set in, he asked himself how he could have allowed them to go without him. A sudden feeling of complete unreality crept over him. The decisions quietly made in this same room a few hours ago now seemed to him unrealistic. He groaned. Under a chair lay a brightly coloured toy of Edgar's, thrown aside in the haste of the departure. As he bent to pick it up, misery and pain gripped him as in a vice. He could barely straighten himself up and with tears streaming down his face, he clutched the edge of the table in a half-kneeling position. Wordlessly he prayed, for the protection of his wife and children, for the Liddells, for the carter, for the night, for the weather, for the road, and even for the pony. He prayed that the Boxers might not be roaming that particular road, and that when morning came that precious cartload of people would have got beyond the reach of those barely human murdering bands. He prayed that Grace would keep her nerve, that the children would not cry nor make any sort of noise that would give away their position. He prayed and prayed and when morning came, he was still half-kneeling and half-lying by the table, exhausted, and to his amazement, hungry. He remembered that he had not eaten at all the previous day.

He was not left alone much longer. Lien-Yi, his beloved Mr Heaven, who had been away in another part of the country, arrived back that morning. His normally smiling face was for once grave and lined with exhaustion, as he told Tom some of the appalling sights he had seen in some country districts. Whole families had been murdered by the roadside, their bodies left unburied and often headless. He did not seem surprised that Grace, the children, and the Liddells had gone, but was dismayed to find Tom still there. '*Taifu*,' he said, 'you should not have stayed. Why did you let them go without you? We would have understood if you had gone.'

Tom tried to explain the doubts and the deliberations of the day before, the intention of Mr Liddell to return, and his own wish not to desert his post and his friends. Mr Heaven did not yield. '*Taifu*,' he said, 'you are wrong. You have not yet fully understood what terrible things are happening to the Christians. I have seen such sights . . . the women and the children . . .' he broke off. 'Wouldn't you rather die with them than stay here?'

Tom could not speak. The agony was rising again in his chest. At that moment, Liu-i came quietly into the house. He busied himself about the dispensary and did not at first speak, but it was obvious that he was suffering some deep emotion. Presently he came up to Tom. '*Taifu*,' he said resolutely, 'You have taught me many things, and I do not forget any of them. You will not have any more patients now, that I can tell you, but anything that happens in all this trouble that needs help, I will deal with. That I promise you.'

'Liu-i,' said Tom at last, 'I cannot leave you here alone. It is known in the town and at the *yamen* that you are a Christian. Should I desert the Mission and leave you here alone in danger? Is that what you expect of me?'

'*Taifu*,' said Liu-i softly, 'do you not understand that if you stay here you are putting us all into greater danger? If you go now, we can go to the mountains and hide as best we can from the Boxers. But if they know you are here, then it is certain they will come and kill us all. Yes, *Taifu*, you must certainly go, for all our sakes.'

Mr Heaven came over and put his arm around Liu-i's shoulders. 'He is right, *Taifu*,' he said. 'We know you came here over the sea, ten thousand miles, to help us. But after all that,' he added with a spark of the old humour, 'we have no wish to give our own heads to the Boxers, and that is what they will do if you stay. You must go today – tonight – after it is dark. I will see to it that all your friends come here this evening to say goodbye. Then you must go, quickly.'

Without waiting for a reply, Mr Heaven walked out. Tom, shaken and still only half-convinced, talked quietly with Liu-i and then started gathering together those few things he thought he could take with him. He was at that time lucky enough to possess a horse, and he decided that to escape on horseback would be the quickest way to catch up the cart. He would wear his Chinese clothes and his queue and he would take to the little known tracks and hide in burial grounds if necessary rather than use the single open road. He carefully laid out on the table two whips and two hats, one a soft trilby hat and the other a Chinese skull cap which he would wear to complete his Chinese appearance.

As he prepared for his departure, his thoughts threatened to become crazed again, imagining what might have already happened to the cartload of frightened women and babies if the screaming blood-stained hordes bore down upon them on that lonely road with their swords upraised. He deliberately occupied himself for the rest of the day, sorting out papers, medical stores, cooking a meal and attending to his horse. News came in every hour or so of fresh horrors seen or reported, of fresh killings and martyrdoms.

As darkness fell, people in twos and threes began to assemble in the little bungalow. About nine o'clock these few Chinese Christians and Tom knelt around the table and commended each other to God's mercy. All were convinced that he must go and they must scatter. Indeed, they promised to do so the moment he had gone. Hand clasped hand, arms were thrown around each other in warm embrace. They looked at one another with new love and appreciation. 'Foreigner' and 'Chinese' were words that no longer had any meaning in this little group as they now saw and touched each others' souls. There were soft murmurs of '*Taifu, taifu*'. The man who was to meet a martyr's death was the one man Tom had thought the weakest in the faith. He died singing as he was cut down.

Tom looked one last time at the place for which he had prayed and hoped and planned so much. He knew he would never see it again. The mud wall around the compound was broken down at the place where he had been preparing to build a little extension to the 'hospital'. It would be all too easy for a mob to rush in and take the place instantly.

As they said their farewells, Tom picked up his hat and strode out of the bungalow without a backward look. His horse was standing saddled at the door. He sprang into the saddle, and rode off on to the plain and made for the distant hills. Behind him fires were raging in the town, and there was the roar of an infuriated, shouting mob. Guns were being fired off, it seemed to him in his direction.

'That's not possible,' thought Tom, 'I look just like any other Chinaman.'

Distractedly, he put his hand up to his head. He knew then why they were firing at him.

He had picked up the wrong hat.

PART II

China

6

Peking – 1901

Tom set sail from England in the autumn of 1901 bound for Peking. He arrived there on the 31st of October. The Boxer Rising had come to a swift end after the Siege of the Embassies, relieved, after forty nine days, by Allied European Forces. The Empress Dowager's savage xenophobia had perforce been extinguished after she had fled Peking in the guise of a peasant, taking the unhappy Emperor with her. She had not dared leave him behind for fear he tried to negotiate with the enemy in her absence. She took refuge in the Western provinces, sending out notices to all Provincial Governors to send tribute to her and then, by sheer audacity and charm, managed to turn her escape into a 'Royal Progress'. This was the only time in her life when she had allowed her four and a half inch long finger nails to be cut. On her return to Peking a year or more later, more than her finger nails were clipped, for she was forced to bow to the victory of the Western powers, and the stringent conditions imposed on China by them. She promptly summoned foreign diplomats and their wives to ceremonies and tea parties in the Palace. She talked of Queen Victoria as her 'sister over the seas' and made reference to China and Britain being 'all one happy family'.

Tom had made good his escape from Chaoyang and had caught up with his family in an emotional reunion at the railhead. His escape, however, had been fraught with danger. He managed to dispose of the trilby hat in a burial ground and was then left without headgear or queue, but wearing his Chinese robes. It was just as he was leading his horse out of the burial ground, picking his way over and around burial mounds and monuments, that he became aware that he was surrounded by Boxers. They formed a circle around him, but were so silent in their movements that the menace in their attitude did not immediately strike him. He stood, holding his horse by the bridle and for a moment nobody moved. He saw the flash of a sword and of scarlet scarves and became aware of their identity and what it presaged for him. He thought his last moment had come. As he prayed silently, one of the Boxers came forward, and to Tom's amazement, intervened his own body between Tom and the leader of the band. 'You will not touch this man except over my dead body!' he said in a loud voice and before the Boxers could do anything he exhorted Tom to remount his horse. 'Ride! ride!' he said, 'if you don't go at once, I cannot protect you.' In a second Tom was back in the saddle and away over the plains lying ahead of him. This time there were no shots fired at him and although he heard some shouting and scuffling behind him, he was not pursued. His mind had been almost paralysed by this encounter, which had happened so suddenly. Now he marvelled at the way he had been able to escape. Although he had not recognised the man who saved him, he realised it must have been one of his own patients. He rode on but began to experience a deadly fatigue. He dared not stop but rode all night, frequently dropping off to sleep in the saddle and only waking up just as he was about to slither off the horse's back. With his exhaustion, he also began to ache all over his body. It was not till after noon of the following day that he reached the railhead and found his anxious family. Construction trains were still running uninterruptedly to Shanghai and the Cochranes and the Liddells were all there on the primitive platform of the railhead. Grace had refused to go on, feeling instinctively that somehow Tom would follow and reach them. Thankfully, they boarded the next train to leave, but by the time they reached the relative safety of Shanghai, Tom was ill with a fever and was shivering and shaking. He referred to this episode only cursorily in later life when he wrote, '*I fell ill in 1900 owing to stress and strain and to malarial infection incurred on my way from Chaoyang to the coast. In consequence at Shanghai I was dangerously ill and delirious and was invalided home as soon as I was able to travel.*' In fact, Tom had developed the most severe form of malarial infection – blackwater fever – and it was only through devoted nursing and care that he survived.

While convalescing in Scotland, he wrote in his diary a little of the thoughts and feelings he had experienced during his illness. He feared he had not stood up as well as he ought to hardship and danger and wondered how he would have fared if he had been put to torture, or loss of wife and children, as many of his colleagues had been. He felt he could however truthfully say, '*If I am faithful to Jesus moment by moment, day by day, when I am well, he will not forsake me when I am ill.*' The thought of the Christians he had left in Chaoyang and all those who had been massacred haunted him. '*Oh my Father, hear my cries about these things,*' he wrote in his physical weakness and returned to the same theme again later on: '*Should I not have said – instead of leaving Chaoyang when they wanted me to do so, "No, I shall stay with you and die with you?"*'

After weeks of convalescence in his native air, however, his strength gradually returned and on the 12th of September, 1900, his diary records: '*I think I am now quite cured of any longing for home and shall be willing to return to China for life. Send me soon, Father.*'

In the meantime he made good use of his time to improve his knowledge of the Chinese language, and read as widely as possible on Oriental subjects, interspersing his activities as his health improved with 'deputation' work for the Mission, fund-raising and preaching.

His prayer for a return to China was granted within a year. During that year the Imperial Court had remained in exile, while the Western powers fell out between themselves, each trying to acquire as many concessions for themselves individually as they could; there was lack of agreement between them as to how heavy the punishments for the Chinese should be, and how much power in future would rest with the different nations. There were complications between Russia and Japan, both wrestling for the possession of Manchuria. America was the only nation not wishing to impose drastically hard indemnities on the Chinese. Eventually, in September, 1901, a Peace Treaty and its conditions were finally signed, giving the Europeans more than they could have hoped for and far more than they had already seized. The Imperial Court began its homeward trek to Peking.

The London Missionary Society, in looking around for a new man in their strategic mission stronghold in Peking, decided to appoint the young doctor who had pioneered so manfully in Mongolia, and had been so providentially spared in the Boxer Rising.

His rapid acquisition of the language (he was now proficient in writing Mandarin Chinese as well as speaking it), his organising skill and obvious ability to co-operate with the Chinese, made the Board firm in its decision to send him to rebuild the Mission Hospital razed to the ground by the Boxers. His job was also to co-ordinate all the medical and educational work undertaken by the LMS in Peking, which had been started as long ago as 1839.

During his long voyage out to China – this time unaccompanied by wife and children whom the Mission had cautiously refused to send back there till times were more 'stable' – Tom had had ample time to think over his new assignment. He had, during his sick leave, acquired a better knowledge of China, its history and religious background. He would not arrive in Peking in such stark ignorance as he had in Mongolia. This time, too, he was being sent, not to a primitive pagan backwater, but to the proud capital city of an empire which had flourished for nearly four thousand years. On the voyage he had written down the history of the various Chinese dynasties, starting with the *Chows* in 1189 BC to the present *Ch'ing* Dynasty, represented by the dreaded Empress-Dowager and the young Emperor, whom she had stripped of all power. An elderly missionary from China, retired in England, had told him that an ancient Manchu prophecy said a woman on the throne would effectively bring the dynasty to an end, and he wondered if this referred to the present Empress-Dowager.

Together with his daily Bible study on board ship, he contrasted the history of the Jews with that of England and China. He marvelled that when Moses led the children of Israel through the wilderness, Chinese laws, literature and religious knowledge excelled that of Egypt. While Homer was composing and singing the *Iliad*, Chinese minstrels were celebrating their ancient heroes whose tombs had already been with them for nearly thirteen centuries. The Chinese had invented the art of printing five hundred years before Caxton was born; they dressed in silk while inhabitants of the British Isles were painting their bodies with woad. The Great Wall was built twenty-two years before Christ was born and contained enough material to build a wall five to six foot high around the globe. While the Israelites were forever fighting their neighbours, killing or being killed by thousands, Chinese armies were learning to conduct parleys and terms of peace under banners of truce bearing two Chinese characters: 'Stop fighting.'

Until the nineteenth century, China had always regarded herself as the centre of the world, even of the universe, and was unaccustomed to any other nation claiming equality. Her emperor was termed the 'Son Heaven'. She virtually regarded the 'dwarfs' of Japan as sub-human, and expected all Western countries to be automatic tribute-bearers acknowledging fealty to her Emperor. England was conceived of as being a tiny island, the property of the Dutch, and incapable of being a world power. Ignorance of Britain's colonising and Empire-building gradually led to dismay followed by fear, as by the middle of the century it slowly began to dawn upon the Chinese that the Western powers were capable of annexing their territory, fighting and winning battles on Chinese soil, opening and controlling ports of trade under their own jurisdiction, and imposing vast sums of money as indemnities for damage done to 'their' property, on the Chinese Government. In many places, notably in Canton, the British lived in sealed-off enclaves in a thoroughly British life-style of luxury and sport, employing Chinese servants but ignoring, often with insults, the upper-class Chinese altogether.

At the same time as the British were developing the opium trade, fiercely resisted in the first place in many Chinese quarters including the Government itself, forcing it upon the nation latterly with corruption and guile, the nations of the West were sending in their Christian missionaries, to teach a foreign religion alien to all that the Chinese held dear. One minister at the Imperial Court was heard to exclaim, 'You foreigners come with opium in one hand and Jesus in the other!' The first mission station in the Province of Honan was closed by a riot in which the infuriated mob drove out the missionaries, crying after them, 'You burnt our Palace! You killed our Emperor! You poison our people and now you come to teach us virtue!'

The people of Canton denounced the guilt of England in these words: 'All the fuel in the Empire would not suffice to purify their (the British) crimes nor would the vast ocean be enough to wash out our resentment.'

In the mounting tension of dread and dislike of the foreigner which had led irresistibly to the Boxer movement, any scientific knowledge or achievement which the West could bring to open up the country to Western 'progress' was ignored or resisted. The introduction of railways and the telegraph system in particular was resented and feared. To the good Confucian, the past meant everything, and any attempt to modernise or change national life cut at the roots all firmly held beliefs. Ancestor worship was threatened and the thread of continuity from generation to generation was liable to be broken by an importation of foreign ideas.

As Tom neared the end of his voyage, he had come to the conclusion that his own country's sins and reputation were going to prove his greatest stumbling block. Justly or unjustly, missionaries were identified with their countrymen, and had to bear their share of China's odium for the deeds and the example set by the Western powers. Once more he was glad that he had trained in medicine and that it was within his power to rectify in however small a way some of the damage done to a proud people. He was resolved to root out, wherever he found it, any lingering belief amongst the Chinese people, that medical missionaries practiced any sort of black magic, or had ever been guilty of mutilating or harming anybody in their practice of medicine.

Although the Mission Hospital had been razed to the ground in Peking, it was the Boxers alone who had done this, and Tom knew that in a small way the Hospital had had a good name amongst the inhabitants of Peking. Dr Lockhart, the first missionary to be sent to China by the LMS, had started his work in Canton, moved to Hankow, and finally had arrived in Peking in the year 1861, travelling just as Tom had done himself in Mongolia four years earlier, in a springless cart, unknown and friendless. Nevertheless, he had built the hospital known as the 'Free Healing Hospital'. He had been succeeded by Dr Dudgeon and in the forty years of its existence, the hospital had treated about one million and a half patients. 'There must be some well-wishers alive,' thought Tom, 'who have benefitted from the hospital's treatment and would welcome its rebuilding.'

When Tom reached Peking, history repeated itself in a strange fashion. Instead of Lien-Yi ('Mr Heaven') coming to his aid on arrival, it was Doctor Li Hsiao Ch'uan who greeted him and showed him around. This Chinese doctor had worked at the hospital until the day it was destroyed by the Boxers. On a cold morning in early November he took Tom to view the remains of the building. 'Look!' he said, 'after forty years we are reduced to this!' He pointed to the pile of rubble which was all that remained of the hospital, and two partially burnt poles which had stood for about two centuries, marking the site of the temple which had been originally acquired for hospital purposes in 1865. The Boxers had tried to burn these poles, but had not succeeded. 'It is a good

The Duchess Te and Dr Tom Cochrane at the tea ceremony whereby the Doctor became officially 'brother-in-law' to the Duchess.

The Empress-Dowager Tzu-Hsi.

The subscription list of donations to the PUMC, headed by the Empress-Dowager's signature.

H E Grand Councillor Na T'ung.

Opening ceremony of The PUMC in 1906. Empress-Dowager's representative, H E Na T'ung, is on the front row, seventh from the left.

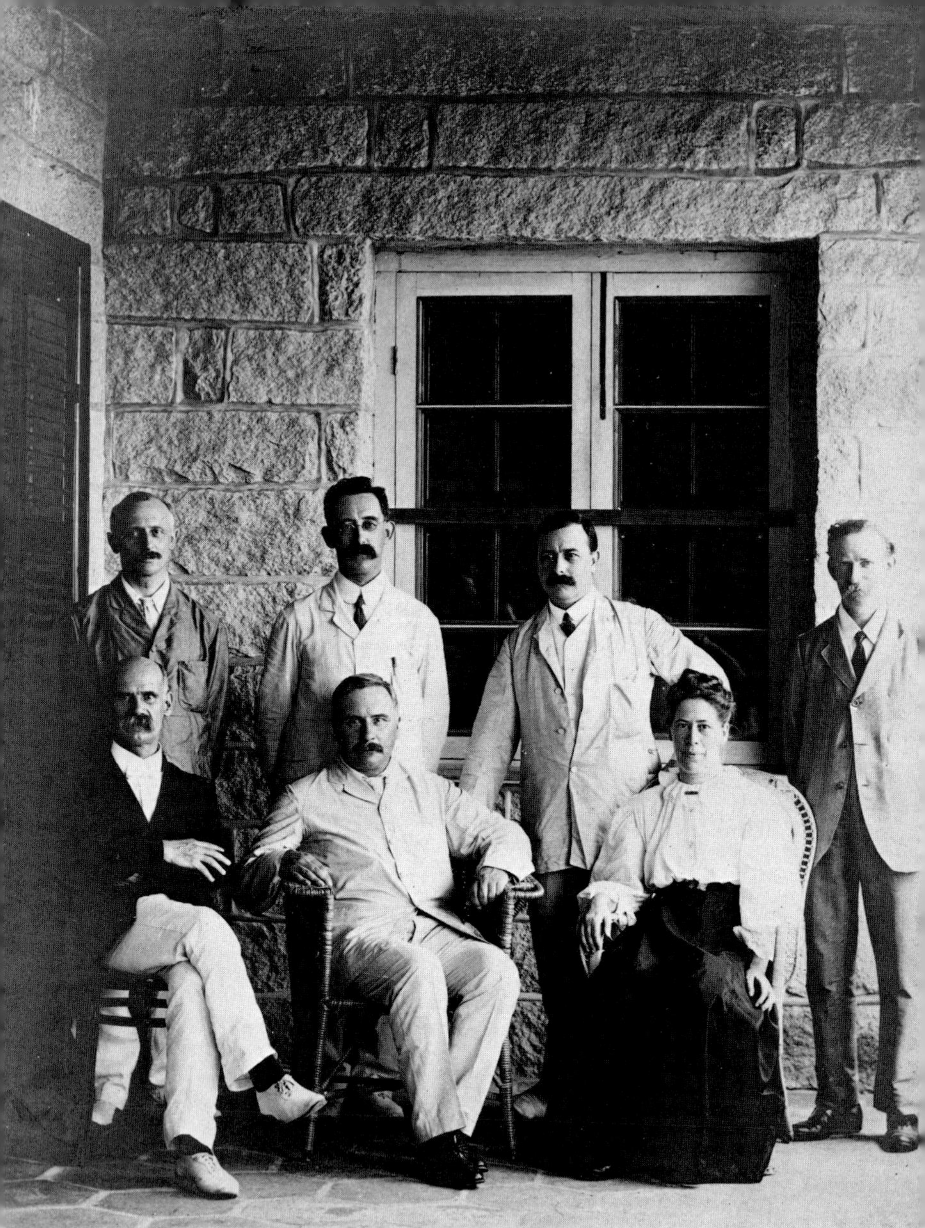

The staff at the PUMC (Dr Cochrane on back row second right; Mrs Cochrane, front row).

In-patients on the women's side of the Hospital (1910).
(The left window leads into the women's wards; the middle window leads into the women's Bible class-room; beyond the wall on the right is the chapel.)

Top: The original PUMC building (1906).
Bottom: First graduating class PUMC (1910–11).

Union Medical College

PEKING

ESTABLISHED WITH IMPERIAL SANCTION AND REGISTERED BY THE IMPERIAL BOARD OF EDUCATION.

The Degree of DOCTOR of MEDICINE is hereby conferred on

Wu San-yüan

who has been found by the Examiners of the College to be duly qualified in the Science and Art of Medicine, and in the Science and Art of Surgery.

In witness whereof the following Seal and signatures are affixed:-

Thos. Cochrane, Principal Union Medical College

W. Hopkyn Rees, Chairman Board of Managers

H. H. Lowry, President Peking University

協和醫學堂

北京

欽命特設學部立案為發給文憑事照得學生吳三元年三十二歲係直隸省故城縣人於光緒三十二年正月由本醫學堂考取入堂肄習各科醫學並按日隨同教習至醫院臨診各症現屆五年期滿於本學堂所定課程均已肄習完畢經 學部派員會同本監督考課長辦各科教習分別考試該生於醫學內外科各門及臨症實驗分數均能及格足以充醫學博士之選為此合行發給文憑以昭信守須至文憑者

協和醫學堂 監督科齡

協和教育會 會長瑞思義

滙文大學堂 監督劉海瀾

協和醫學堂圖記

A College Degree Certificate from the PUMC.

The professorial staff at the PUMC (Dr Cochrane is the third from the right, front row).

A group of in-patients.

Dr Li (Senior Chinese staff).

Medical students who were on plague duty in Tientsin with the Sanitary Police.

A wealthy patient in Peking.

Part of the PUMC premises as rebuilt by the Rockefeller Foundation (1915–21).

The great 'foreign' *Taifu* who brought spiritual truth and Western medicine to the 'poorest of the poor' and to the Dragon Throne.

omen,' the Chinese said, 'that the poles remain.' This comforted Tom and confirmed his hope that there still were well-wishers amongst the population of Pekin.

Dr Li Hsiao Ch'uan excused himself and left Tom to wander about on his own. Peking showed the wounds inflicted on it, and although it was over a year since the Allies had marched in and fighting had stopped, it presented a scene of desolation and destruction. Over acres of ground, especially in the business and Legation sectors, buildings had been razed to the ground and were now just piles of brick and rubble. There had been much looting not only by the Boxers but by the Western powers and the Russians. One city gate with its huge superstructure of carved magnificence had been burnt down. The beautiful Summer Palace, outside Peking, previously pillaged and burnt down by the French and the British in 1860 and then carefully and expensively restored by the Empress-Dowager, had been looted and damaged once again. Here and there in the city were posters written in English by Chinese owners of shops or restaurants begging the kind English 'Sirs' not to do them any harm. 'We are all good men here,' said one placard pathetically. Another simply said, 'No looting. Nothing left.' Very little restoration of buildings or houses had been attempted.

The site of the city of Peking dated back some centuries before the birth of Christ, but it had not been made the capital of the whole Empire till Kublai Kahn established his Court there in 1264. Although the city, as Tom saw it that cold and frosty day in November 1901, was not on exactly the same site, and remains of ancient sites were still to be found outside the city walls, the arrangement of streets and gates was to all intents and purposes the same as they had been in the thirteenth century. Exclusive of suburbs, the city was over twenty miles in circumference and consisted of four cities –

1. The 'Forbidden City', which was the residence of the Imperial Court.
2. The 'Imperial City', which surrounded The 'Forbidden City' and was partially closed.
3. The 'Tartar City' enclosing the 'Imperial City'.
4. The 'Chinese City' south of the 'Tartar City' and extending a little beyond it west and east. The east, west and south walls of the 'Chinese City' measured eight miles. There were seven gates to the 'Chinese City' and nine to the 'Tartar City'.

All these quarters of Peking Tom was to get to know intimately.

In this city of great contrasts, beautiful, graceful, palatial houses, in grounds laid out with exquisite artistry, stood amongst tumble-down, wretched slum dwellings no better than the squalid hovels Tom had known in Chaoyang. Indeed, he could almost believe he was back there because of the hordes of beggars who clustered around him, half-naked, many of them bare-footed and some bearing signs of frostbite and obviously starving, begging for some relief from their miserable plight. What pointed up their condition even more than in Mongolia, where nearly everybody was poor, was the appearance of wealthy individuals clad in gorgeous coloured silks, lined with luxurious furs, who rode around the city in brilliantly painted carts, or were being carried in sedan chairs, borne along by as many as four bearers, and with a couple of mounted outriders in bright livery. The sedans were covered in materials of rich velour or velvet. The occupants passed these unfortunate beggars, some blind, some limbless, and all emaciated by hunger, without a single glance. Tom was reminded of the indifference shown to the headless corpses, newly executed, by the inhabitants of Chaoyang on the night of his first arrival.

With a sinking heart and a distinct feeling of *déjà vu*, Tom began to think that, as a doctor, he was much in the same position as he had been in Chaoyang, where for three years he had expended so much of his physical energy in ministering individually to the poor, neglected and disease-ridden people of Mongolia. Then a fresh tide of resolution surged through him. God and the Boxers had relieved him of that drudgery, and with the mandate to rebuild the LMS hospital, here was a new situation and climate of opinion. He remembered his conviction before he had to flee Chaoyang, that the best use of his gifts and the best thing for the Chinese nation would be to train young Christian Chinese in modern Western medicine. He must not hark back to Mongolia, except to remember the lessons it had taught him as a solitary doctor in a huge expanse of territory. Here he was not being left alone and remote from the rest of the world to face inimical and repressive 'enemies'. Here was a new opportunity to gain the co-operation of a defeated nation, whose ruler had been obliged to submit to the hated foreigners and to make far-reaching concessions to them.

The Peace Treaty of September 17, 1901, had imposed a punitive indemnity upon China (far more than she could ever pay); foreign troops were now allowed to be stationed between Tientsin and Peking, and to be garrisoned in an official Legation quarter; any officials who neglected to suppress anti-foreign plots or societies were liable to be dismissed from their posts forever. State examinations were to be suspended for five years in all places where foreigners had been attacked. Missionaries were to be allowed to live and teach freely throughout China.

Despite all this, Tom knew that if he wanted to succeed in his plan to found a college for the training of Chinese medical students alongside the hospital, he would need official sanction and patronage. So why, he asked himself, not go to the very top?

He began to think about the Empress Dowager, Tzu-Hsi. He had read much about China's dynastic history going back to the distant past while on his return voyage to China, but he did not know much about its present ruler. He knew Tzu-Hsi had originally been a concubine of the Emperor Hsien-Feng and had survived the death of her husband, who had died in 1861, and her son who died of smallpox when he came of age. During his minority she had been co-Regent with the former Empress, who had died in 1881. Tzu-Hsi had then become sole Regent until her nephew, the Emperor Kuang Hsu, appointed heir to the Throne came of age seven years later and her Regency ended. Tom had heard that Kuang Hsu's disgrace and downfall had come in 1898 when, under the influence of the 'Reformers', the young Emperor had tried to introduce a form of Christianity into China through a series of Edicts. This attempt had appalled the Empress Dowager who was totally opposed to any sort of change. The Emperor had conspired with Yuan Shih, an outstanding Army Commander, to cut off her still remaining power. But the plot had rebounded on him through the latter's treachery, after which Tzu-Hsi had seized her nephew and imprisoned him. She had then issued an Edict saying he was too ill to continue to rule and had asked her to resume her rulership. She had now been on the Throne of China for over forty years almost uninterruptedly, and according to Dr Li Hsiao Ch'uan, who had talked to Tom on these matters the previous evening, she was unlikely to modify her previous attitudes very much in the future. Dr Li had mentioned also that she relied heavily on her Grand Eunuch, who hated the young Emperor. He had intimated also that the Grand Eunuch played on Tzu-Hsi's hatred and that it was he who had really instigated the Boxer Rising. Between them, they constituted a strong front against change and Dr Li thought this example and influence would continue.

Tom carefully considered all the conditions now imposed on the

Manchu rulers. Although forced to agree to the terms of the Peace Treaty, the Empress-Dowager could not, in Tom's opinion, possibly have changed her inner and lifelong dislike and hatred of foreigners. Would she merely pay lip service to the changes now imposed on her régime and try at some future time to start again her endless plotting and scheming if the present controls loosened? Whichever way things went, Tom thought it was highly desirable that British missionaries should now demonstrate to her that they, if not their compatriots, had the welfare of her nation at heart. Even if her character could not be changed, would it not be a great gain if her genuine sympathy could be gained? One thing was on his side. The London Missionary Society hospital had had a reasonably good name at Court. The young Emperor had on one occasion sent one of his courtiers to it, with a carbuncle measuring nine by six inches, saying, 'Go to the Mission doctor. He is the only one who can deal with a case like this.' But foreign doctors had never been allowed to enter the precincts of the Palace, and there had never been any official acknowledgment of their competence or their rôle. They were mostly consulted when native doctors had failed. Besides which, the Empress-Dowager herself was a keen diagnostician and prescriber and had been known to impose her prescriptions upon members of the Court – one of them had contained one hundred ingredients – and was ruthless in her insistence that they be taken. She was at least genuinely interested and curious about medical matters. Already a new European hospital had been built in Peking since the end of the Boxer Rising, but it was a condition that religious teaching would not be allowed in it. It was therefore most important that 'his' hospital should not be restricted in this way, that it be staffed only by Christian doctors and that the training given to the Chinese be initially in their own language and strictly in line with Christian traditions of healing.

Historically, Tom realised that his appointment to Peking had put him in a strategic position at a crucial hour. But for what purpose? Merely to rebuild a small hospital and resume a forty-year old work which had been ruthlessly destroyed in its entirety in an illegal rebellion?

He managed to shake off the beggars swarming around him, gently promising that when he had premises in which to give medical treatment, he would help them to the best of his ability, and slowly returned to the site of the hospital ruins.

He knew what had to be done. Somehow, in restitution for past wrongs done to and in this country, the true spirit of Christ and his compassion must be allowed to flow in such a way that it would be seen and acknowledged by those in power and by those oppressed.

He slowly clambered up to the top of the heap of rubble, and looked north-west to the yellow-tiled roofs of the Imperial Palace. He thought again of the authority and power which the autocratic throne exerted over the great and ancient Empire of China.

'*Under a sudden impulse*,' he wrote when describing his introduction to Peking, '*I prayed that God would somehow enable me to touch one of the oldest thrones in the world.*'

7

The Grain Shop

It was not Tom's habit to sit around and wait for prayer to be answered. His natural impulse was to get on with whatever was next to hand and leave his requests to a higher wisdom than his own. Nevertheless, he had to start somewhere.

As he clambered down from the pile of rubble, he noticed, adjacent to the site of the ruined hospital, a disused grainshop and behind it a row of stables occupied by a couple of mules. On the face of it, these premises did not seem a suitable stop-gap until the new hospital was built, nor a promising step in the direction of the Dragon Throne, but nonetheless Tom felt the urge to make enquiries about them. When, next day, he explained his need for a dispensary and surgery and offered to rent both the grainshop and the stables, he was surprised at the enthusiastic reception he received and the offer of their use free. Tom thought humorously that the Lord intended to keep him humble and was not going to allow him any illusions of grandeur.

Besides this, he was very grateful for the remission of rent. As he wrote at the end of that year, '*All this involves me in great financial responsibilities. The Society gives me a grant of forty pounds a year for my work. My wages alone amount to between eighty and ninety pounds (a year) and over and above this I have to provide for my own drugs, instruments and dressings, general hospital utensils, coals, etc.*'

Within a couple of days the mules were turned out and Tom moved in. The grainshop was even more dilapidated than his original rooms in Chaoyang. There were just as many rats in the ceiling and his operating table was a discarded door laid on trestles. In no time at all, Tom was receiving the beggars, the homeless and the outcast. Some were leprous, all were filthy and they brought with them every kind of disease known to China. '*I did what I could,*' he wrote, '*to make the operating room a little less dangerous, and soon after my arrival I was doing all kinds of major operations with marvellously good results. My in-patients were housed in what had formerly been the stables from which the mules were turned out and the walls whitewashed.*' Tom was in practice again, except that none of his patients had any money and were even more wretched than the poor Mongols he had served in Chaoyang. Many of them had no home at all, not even a roofless one, and the winter in Peking was no less cruel than it had been in Mongolia.

One man who came to see him with severe frostbite lived in a dog kennel and his only cover was a piece of old frayed matting, which did not completely cover him. His legs and feet had been exposed to frostbite and Tom had to amputate them below the knee and fit the man out with wooden legs. Happily his patient was eventually able to earn a living and live in one room of a proper house.

From the beginning of his work in these temporary premises, Tom had the support of his new friend, Dr Li Hsiao Ch'uan, who gave him all his spare time and much useful advice. He also found Tom some Chinese assistants who had worked at the old hospital and were glad to help him with the in-patients in the 'mules quarters'.

Only one thing had greatly upset Tom on his arrival in Peking. At Chaoyang he had been accustomed to squalor and hardship, but not to separation from his family. On November 2nd, he wrote to the LMS –

'*You will be glad to hear of my safe arrival after a very pleasant voyage. At Singapore I got my first letter of welcome from Peking accompanied by the enquiry "Why are you not bringing your wife from England? There is no reason whatever why she should not come," and all along the way after that I was being asked the same question. I felt bad about it, I can tell you, seeing I had been so anxious to have her – and so was she anxious to come – and so disconsolate at being left behind.*'

Indeed, he had nearly written in protest to the Directors of the London Missionary Society requesting that Grace be sent out immediately, but tactfully he had delayed until he had seen for himself what conditions in Peking were like. Now he concluded –

'. . . *As for risk there is absolutely none. Ladies are going* even into the country, *and as for accommodation, things are not what they were before the buildings were destroyed, but we have four times the accommodation we had when we went first to Chaoyang, and besides that we have been invited to stay with friends close by if we feel cramped . . .*'

Finally Tom insisted firmly that Grace and the three children be sent out as soon as they could be made ready and that details of their sailing be wired to him: '*Address your wire "Cochrane, Peking" and simply give the steamer's name*' he wrote optimistically – and as an afterthought: '*Please also pay my wife the usual outfit money. It will be five years since she had any and the children have never had any at all.*'

There was some further delay in Grace's departure, but by 17th February, 1902, Tom was writing wryly: '*I am leaving in a week or so to meet my wife at Shanghai as she will need my help to come up north. I have got the house here in fair order for her reception. The rooms are small but the accommodation is quite sufficient in the meantime. If you want to make some people content with their lot, send them to such a place as Chaoyang for a few years and you will have no trouble with them afterwards!*'

As he made preparations to go to Shanghai to meet Grace and the children, a strange incident occurred which forcibly reminded him of something that, deeply immersed as he had been in his 'beggars' dispensary' and the plans for financing and rebuilding the hospital, he had for the time being almost forgotten.

He was walking through the streets of the Imperial City one morning at the end of February when he heard a wild clatter of hooves behind him and the sound of the wheels of a cart travelling much too fast. He swung round to see a cart painted in the bright colours of the Imperial Court, swaying from side to side with its pony totally out of control. The driver was struggling unsuccessfully to pull the pony up, while an outrider in bright livery was trying to overtake the cart and bring the pony to a halt. The cart swerved madly from one side of the narrow street to the other while its occupant, a man dressed in silks and furs, fought to keep his seat. Tom took a step backwards as the cart swept by and as he did so, the occupant of the cart was thrown out and landed with considerable force at Tom's feet. He was badly winded and it took him some time to struggle to his feet with Tom's help, panting and shaken. He managed nonetheless to maintain his dignity and allowed Tom to brush him down and retrieve his cap with the ruby-coloured button which proclaimed him an Imperial Prince (The streets of Peking were always filthy and the cap had fallen straight into a dunghill). Tom felt he had better introduce himself before he offered any further assistance. It was unlikely that this Prince had broken any bones or he would not have been able to get to his feet.

'I am Dr Thomas Cochrane of the London Missionary Society,' he said. 'Is there anything you would like me to do for you?' By this time a small crowd had collected and were gaping at the sight of a man in foreign clothing speaking to a high official of the Imperial Court in public and even, apparently, offering him help.

The man regarded Tom with interest, taking in the European clothes and the voice with its flawless Chinese intonation. He was evidently impressed by Tom's looks and manner. He bowed slightly to him, thanked him, saying all was well with him and accepted his help in climbing back into the cart, which by now had been retrieved. As he seated himself, he turned and again directed a small bow in Tom's direction. Tom bowed deeply in return.

As the cart clattered off at a respectable pace, Tom, slightly dazed himself by this sudden and violent encounter, addressed himself to the nearest bystander.

'To whom,' he asked in Chinese, 'have I had the pleasure of addressing myself?'

The man stared back at him, as did others in the crowd, in astonishment. It seemed to them impossible that this foreigner, if he lived in Peking and spoke Chinese so perfectly, should not recognise the man he had just helped back into his cart.

'Do you not know, Sir?' he replied. 'That is one of Her Majesty's most treasured Ministers. That, Sir, is the great Prince Su!'

As Tom strode down the street, he chuckled inwardly. Although he had never before actually seen a member of the Imperial Court, he had certainly heard of Prince Su. He had heard from Dr Li that Prince Su was one of the most influential and wealthy men in the Empire. He had not sided with the Boxers and yet had managed to retain the confidence of the Empress-Dowager after she had returned from exile. Prince Su was a Mongol Prince married to a *Manchu* Princess. He had a beautiful estate and palace to the south of Peking, where his ancestors had tombs going right back to the days of the Mongolian Dynasty. One ancestor had his servant buried alongside him who had voluntarily and valiantly offered to die in order to be with his master. The Palace had escaped being ravaged by the Boxers. When in Peking, the Prince had his own rooms in the Imperial Palace.

When Tom reached his own small box-like house, he went in and sat down. He wanted to think out quietly the implications of the morning's incident. As he thought back over the past few weeks, he was amazed at the sequence of events. First, he had prayed what many people would have thought a presumptuous prayer. He, a 'foreign devil', hated by the Empress-Dowager, had asked to be allowed to touch the Dragon Throne. Only a few months earlier, the Empress-Dowager would have willingly connived at his death through the Boxers, not only because he was a Westerner but because he was a Christian. But he had prayed for her patronage for his plans to help the Chinese through medical education; he had even prayed for her help in bringing the light of the Gospel to the rulers of the nation themselves. The Emperor had been savagely punished for trying to make just such a change in the life and education of the nation by his terrible Aunt.

After the Boxer Rising, Tom felt that Christian missionaries could never be sure of a permanent foothold in China. Therefore the need was paramount to build up one body of Chinese Christians who would become one Church of Christ in China, that could survive and expand without dependence on foreigners.

What next? After today's incident, was he now one step nearer to the Throne? He did not know. But the extreme accuracy with which Prince Su had landed at his feet had made it a strange experience indeed. If this had been the Lord's doing, then he had better wait and see what more would happen. He remembered Moses' injunction to the Israelites on a certain traumatic occasion: '*Stand still*,' Moses had said, '*and see the salvation of the Lord.*' Perhaps this 'standing still and seeing' was the heart of prayer. He felt there was now a current running in his life over which he had no control. But he could expect answers.

He decided that he would demonstrate his faith in God to himself the following day. He would walk three times round the 'Forbidden City' and he would pray at every step. If the heathen of Mongolia could prostrate themselves and travel on their bellies for miles on a pilgrimage to one of their sacred places, could he not in turn deepen and strengthen his own prayers to the one true

God for his Chinese children? He would undertake this pilgrimage of love before Grace and the children arrived and he would do it the very next day. It was an arduous and exacting task – the 'Forbidden City' was fourteen miles in circumference, and Tom Cochrane was not the most robust of men, but he was still only thirty eight years old, and determination ran deep in him.

He went to bed with a glowing sense of confidence. Something quite extraordinary had happened that day, for which he could thank God. And the long separation from his family was all but over. It was six months since he had seen them and the boys must have grown considerably. He felt that Grace would be pleased at the more spacious accommodation they had in Peking, and there was hope for something even better in the future.

As to the lowliness of his present dispensary and 'hospital', they were only a temporary expedient, and when the new hospital was built he hoped it would be spacious and have all the latest equipment. A sudden pang went through him. Was he becoming too ambitious in a worldly sense? He must always be on guard against this temptation. Perhaps he should not give up this beggars' refuge even when the new hospital was built. To some of these outcasts the stables were a paradise. He grew sleepy and a vagrant thought kept eluding him. What *was* he trying to remember? Something to do with a stable . . . paradise . . . a Prince? Of course, that was it. Jesus himself was born in a stable. How could he have forgotten that all these months? Everything was all right. '*A servant is not above his master*,' not even in China, let alone Peking, with all its architectural wonders and grandeur and magnificence. He had 'brushed down' a Prince of the blood royal that day. But what had the 'Prince of Peace' done all his working life but lift people out of the mire, 'brush them down,' and restore them to themselves and to God?

The next day he walked three times around the 'Forbidden City', praying for the Court, its rulers, its officials, its princes, princesses, and its eunuchs. He prayed for his fellow missionaries and doctors. He prayed for the whole of China. He prayed especially for Dr Li whom he was leaving in charge till his return.

Two days later, he left for Shanghai.

8

Confucius and Kipling

As Grace settled happily into their new Chinese quarters, and the children rushed excitedly from room to room and had to be restrained from running out into the filthy, germ-laden streets of Peking, Tom was carefully deepening his knowledge of the ways of the Chinese upper classes, with whom he had had no previous contact. He felt his need to know more and understand better the moral and social implications of their inherited beliefs. He was now beginning to meet the educated Chinese. If God were to allow him to touch the Dragon Throne, he must learn about the historical traditions of Chinese rulership beforehand. He wanted, if questioned, to be able to give a clear answer as to why, as a Westerner, he was in China and what he thought he could contribute of value to the nation.

His first professional contact apart from the 'beggars' dispensary' was with the wife of a highly placed Government official who had invited him, through Dr Li, to visit her in their luxurious Chinese home. Tom was ushered into her presence with deep bows and apparent respect towards himself by a male servant, who had obviously been briefed by his master to observe all Chinese ceremony. After bowing to her, Tom approached the lady, dressed in high *Manchu* fashion, politely asking her to give him her hand and allow him to take her pulse. She reluctantly held out her hand, but almost immediately withdrew it, and taking Tom's own hand in hers she deliberately and with good aim spat into his palm. Tom, confused and wondering what *étiquette* he had neglected to observe, bowed and backed away. In face of this affront, he decided not to wipe the saliva from his hand in her presence. It was obviously the husband's and not the wife's initiative which had brought him on this visit. He wondered if the insult was premeditated or just an impulse born of long distrust and animosity to the foreigner. He must consult Dr Li on the matter. He let the saliva dry in his palm till he got outside the house, and returned home thoughtfully.

Another patient of wealth and some standing sent for him in a great hurry to attend his wife. 'She has a very bad temper,' he confided to Tom, 'and she is my fifth wife. I don't really mind if she dies, so do not make too much effort to cure her. I have to ask you to see her for the sake of appearance. But my family burial ground is full and if she dies, it will mean buying a new plot of land.'

Tom took these Chinese attitudes and all that was implied spiritually in them into his morning 'hour' which now often began an hour earlier and extended into two hours. The children were sometimes noisy in the early morning and more and more often Tom would steal out of the house at daybreak and make for some quiet spot where he could find solitude and commune with God uninterruptedly. He came to like a certain spot in the Western hills where there was a large white rock. He scratched the word *Bethel* on it and here he often read, wrote and prayed.

While on his way out from England, he had carefully made out a summary of Chinese history and beliefs. He considered that every missionary should have this kind of knowledge to help him in his daily life amongst the Chinese.

The fact which most intrigued Tom was that the Chinese claimed to have a pre-historic mythical Golden Age, where man was sinless and earth life perfect. No crimes were committed and everyone lived in happiness and without fear. Nothing was ever lost. Although there were no traceable links with biblical Old Testament history, this idea coincided with the Garden of Eden and its innocence.

The Chinese believed in a 'First Cause' which had created the world out of chaos three million years ago. This 'First Cause' then separated into *yen* and *ying*, male and female, or heaven and earth. After this, man was created and thus a coalition of three powers, heaven, earth, and mankind, was formed, all of which acted harmoniously with one another.

Shangti or *Tien* was the name for the one supreme Ruler of heaven and earth. The opening sentence of history declared that the great Emperor Shun offered the 'customary sacrifice' to God, implying that even at this remote period, it had become customary. There were no idols or images of any kind. There was no temple to God or heaven, but anywhere and any time an altar could be erected on which to offer a sacrifice to God, who was presumed to be omni-present. There were no terms to signify sin or holiness in a spiritual sense. Sacrifices were made in gratitude, to avert calamity or to procure blessing. Sacrifices on behalf of others were completely absent. The departed great or good ones were in the presence of God.

'*Religion*,' wrote Tom in his 'Day Book', '*has ever been closely associated with mankind of all sorts of mentality and all degrees of education and civilisation. The worship of the unseen powers behind the great mysterious visible universe is influenced by fear and hope, and ethics become associated with religion and beliefs constitute creed. Probably no religious system known to us can be traced continually in its completeness . . . so far . . . as that of China.*' Tom thought he could see certain similarities in the approach of ancient Chinese worship of the one true God to that of Old Testament history. But he went on, '*There has, however, been no Chinese New Testament evolving out of the past. If anything, there is evidence of deterioration and a materialisation of the spirituality of the ancient type. Had the story of the original religion of China been generally known, the theory that the spiritual form of religion is the result of a long process of evolution from an original image worship would not have been so readily broached.*'

It would be hard if not impossible to say when this deterioration and materialisation began. But at a certain stage in history, ancient records give evidence of a belief in a spirit world somewhere between heaven and earth inhabited by *knei* (demon) and *shen* (spirit) who were interchangeable deities of a lower order, though they were always described as subordinate to God and engaged in carrying out his will. Whether they could be compared to biblical angels was another matter. There was no Chinese belief in disobedient or fallen angels who could beguile humanity as in the Genesis story. Gradually, however, the belief arose that the great and good departed could come and go and interfere in the affairs of their descendents. It was but a step from this to the building of temples called the '*Maio*', dedicated to departed ancestors, whose worship began to plague and bind the Chinese to religious practices which put them forever in thrall. Idol worship can be traced back to about the same time.

'*Whence came the monotheism of the Jews and of China*?' Tom asked in his diary. '*Polytheism (worship of many gods) and idolatory existed everywhere except in Israel and China. Was there a common origin*?' Leaving the question unanswered, he went on to note the differences in the spiritual history of the two nations. The Jewish system, he felt, was characterised by a deeper spirituality than the Chinese. The heart sorrow for sin and the joy of forgiveness were absent from Chinese monotheism. The Chinese had certainly come at a later stage to worship inferior deities, though these were still subordinated to the one supreme God, whereas Jewish beliefs in the purity and holiness of God forbade the worship of any other deity. The worship of the golden calf, Baal worship and other idolatorous habits had led God's people astray in Jewish history and they were punished for it. It was impossible to say exactly at what point the purity of the ancient Chinese religion had been adulterated.

The teaching of sages such as Lao-Tze, with his 'Way' – followed by Confucius, born in 551 BC but who actually lived one thousand years after the beginning of Confucianism and then Mencius, held up the ideal of virtue. Idol worship was not, and never had been any part of Confucianism. What was taught and handed down was a concept of moral order and a theory of human government, especially as applied to statecraft, which appeared to be singularly adapted to the people of China. It was one of the priceless assets which the Chinese had accepted from antiquity. The Emperor was to be worshipped, but the Emperor himself – named 'Son of Heaven' – had to worship publicly once a year. He represented the people before the 'Most High God'. Thus the first of six great dynasties, starting about 1120 BC coincided with the initial steps into civilisation for China, who had solemnly believed that their 'Middle Kingdom' was the centre of the world, and indeed of the Universe.

From the time of the First Dynasty – the *Chows* – and throughout the ensuing five to the moment when Tom was writing, Chinese civilisation had made fairly unbroken progress in arts, science, astronomy, writing, printing and rulership. Pristine innocence had by then obviously been lost. There had been both good and bad emperors, some of them poets, some powerful and peace-loving, some warlike and aggressive. Despite the varied characters and fortunes of the emperors, the central idea of their unique position in the life of China and its vast empire was never abandoned. The present Empress-Dowager, however, was the first woman to occupy the Dragon Throne and actually to rule the country; and she had only reached the Throne through murder and stealth.

The present Dynasty – the *Ch'ings* or *Manchus* – had come to power when the previous Emperor of the *Ming* Dynasty (1370–1650 AD) had committed suicide after military defeat and treachery. It had had ten emperors, the second and fourth of which had been great rulers. One of them had tried to stop foot-binding of girls, but had not succeeded. From its earliest days, this *Ch'ing* Dynasty had enforced the queue or pigtail in men, a habit originally loathed by the Chinese who had considered it both a badge of servitude and effeminate. It had, however, ultimately been accepted. The *Manchus*, being themselves an usurping power, were certainly not universally liked or respected in China. Their inability to do anything but look back to the past for direction and guidance throughout the nineteenth century had weakened them considerably. The present ruler had ruthlessly suppressed the young Emperor's dream of abolishing the Civil Service State examinations, which were based entirely on a knowledge of Confucius' teaching and the classics. This system tended to turn young men into soulless bureaucrats, and eventually into full-blown mandarins or magistrates whose humanity was often fettered by a legalism of outlook unsoftened by any sort of compassion. The Chaoyang mandarin had demanded of Tom just before the family's flight, that he surrender any pistols or arms he possessed. This demand had been presented in a manner which was a veiled threat, as Tom had been quick to note. He actually possessed no arms, but from that moment he had known he would get no protection from the Mandarin of Chaoyang.

So far as rulership was concerned, the Empress-Dowager, Tzu-Hsi, still appeared to have sublime self-confidence despite being obliged to submit at last to Western influences. The Emperor, her nephew, whom she had stripped of all power and humiliated beyond all reason, still bore the official title 'the Son of Heaven'. She had meanwhile adopted for herself the following titles: 'Loving-hearted and Fortunate, Upright and Aiding, Happy and Careful, Bright and Pleasant, Earnest and True, Longlived and Serious, Reverent and Good, Exalted and Brilliant, Empress Grand

Dowager.' 'Merciful', however was not a title she laid claim to. She inspired terror in many people, especially the young Emperor. And she was reputed to have a squad of floggers at all times in public in attendance upon her and to mete out punishment summarily to anyone she thought merited it. The Grand Eunuch was her private executioner.

Tzu-Hsi was known to be a highly superstitious woman down to every detail of her daily life. No doubt this trait had been inculcated into her early life by the degenerate aspects of *Tao-ism*. This was sad, Tom reflected, as its philosophy was pure (he recalled that 'the Way' was a term also used about the early Christians' teaching). Only vulgar popularisation and misunderstanding of it had caused superstition to arise. As a ruler, however, she was obliged to rely on the maxims of Confucius to lead her, and that meant she must set a good example and must be seen to do so. She must seek the good of the people (according to Confucius) and the peoples' loyalty was dependent on the ruler's devotion to their interests.

Actually, Confucius had never claimed to be more than mere man. He had never posed as a saviour of mankind, nor promised anything to do with everlasting life. Indeed, his words were, '*We have not yet performed our duties to man. How can we perform our duties to spirits? – and not knowing life, how can we know about death*?' Another dismal saying of his was, '*He who has sinned against heaven has no place to pray.*' Confucius' one aim was to restore the Golden Age; yet he died lamenting his failure. The five virtues which he preached were all-important, and he said, when dying: '*When you fail, seek help in yourself.*' Poor Tzu-Hsi, Tom thought, perhaps she had tricked herself into believing she really was all that her self-given titles professed. If ever her self-confidence failed her, whom could she turn to? Confucius had taken away from the Chinese the thought of the one true God which was the greatest possession of their great ancestors. The entire absence of a personal God to whom an individual soul had access and could pray, made all the difference between Confucius' ideals and Jesus' teaching. Jesus had brought to the Jews the new concept of God as Father. Moreover, he had frequently challenged individuals to make costly decisions if they wanted to follow him, and had declared, '*I am the Way, the Truth and the Life.*' He had held out the promise of a coming of the Kingdom of God, and his gospel was in the end to be preached to everybody, regardless of their nationality or status. Earthly power thus received little importance in the sight of God.

It was intensely significant, Tom thought, that Jesus had been born at the junction of East and West, and was uniquely able to understand both. Kipling's line,

> *'Oh, East is East, and West is West, and never the twain shall meet'*

was often quoted as if that were the end of the matter. But the poem went on,

> *'Till earth and sky stand presently at God's great judgment seat'* . . .

and concluded,

> *'But there is neither East nor West, Border, nor Breed, nor Birth*
> *When two strong men stand face to face, though they come from the ends of the earth!'*

That was Kipling's idea. But two strong men facing each other did not necessarily imply unity or even amity. Why had Kipling not ended with an embrace, a reconciliation, a bond of peace? '*We are all one in Christ Jesus*' Paul had written in his highest moments. Tom had experienced this spiritual unity that last night in Chaoyang when all barriers of race and nationality had been broken down. He knew that it could happen. Perhaps it was most likely to occur in moments of common danger or peril. But once the barrier down, and the love of Christ uniting those of different backgrounds, there would be no division between East and West – neither for two strong men, nor two weak women, nor children, nor nations. *But when, Oh Lord,* Tom prayed, *would this time of peace and love and understanding come? When would the healing of the nations take place?*

He prayed and he waited, but nothing came to him; only a strong sense that he must continue to walk by faith – not by sight.

9

The Next Step

Tom's faith, as he himself admitted, was strained as he came into closer touch with the post-Boxer attitude, especially among officials whose relatives had suffered much indignity while Peking had been occupied by foreign troops. One official declared that it would give him great pleasure to make his bed on the skin of a foreigner, and more than once Tom was treated to rude and contemptuous gestures by high-born *Manchu* ladies in ducal houses. '*It was then*,' he wrote, '*that I realised more clearly my audacity in hoping to influence the Empress on the Throne. If anyone had heard me praying thus, they would have thought me mad to ask for such an impossible result of any work that I might do, or any influence I might exert in my medical work in that great conservative stronghold.*'

As he clung to the belief that nothing was impossible with God, he realised that there were East-West divisions in himself which needed healing. To identify more with the Chinese, watch them and learn to understand them, he must think more in Chinese. This did not mean imitating or emulating them; that would be artificial and would not appeal to these shrewd and clever people. He turned to the gospels for new insights. Jesus had taken on himself all the limitations of the human body and was tempted in all points as the rest of mankind, yet without sin. There had been no weaknesses in Jesus. There must be no weaknesses in him if he was to be God's means of blessing these people and of teaching them his nature as LOVE. Neither could they be won to any better beliefs than they already had without this love. Tom gradually became confident that China as a nation could be won for Christ only as Christ was allowed to meet China's deepest needs. Improving the conditions of the poor, the results of sickness and disease, even saving lives and educating the nation in modern scientific thought were not enough by themselves. All actions must be motivated by love and nothing else. A profound peace enveloped him. He felt that in this confused, chaotic country, where much was rotten and much was beginning to change, a spiritual revolution was beginning. New wine was being poured into old wineskins and many of them would burst. Wherever he encountered an anti-Western attitude he must be ready to humble himself and show the love of Christ in return. He must not bring about changes merely to introduce Western ideas and influence for their own sake. He knew of one American mission school where the children were taught exclusively American history and were led to believe that there had been only three great men in the history of the world – Jesus Christ, Abraham Lincoln and George Washington. Of their own culture extending into the infinite past and their own great rulers they were told nothing. Tom cringed when he thought of it.

In contrast to the wealthy lady who had spat into his palm and the man who did not want the expense of burying his fifth wife, he found that most of his poor patients disproved the idea common amongst casual observers, that the Chinese were stolid and indifferent and lacked the milk of human kindness. Many of them would break down in tears while describing their afflictions or those of their family as they felt themselves in the presence of someone who was genuinely sympathising with them and helping them. If family pride or rank inhibited some of the upper-class privileged Chinese from showing signs of being human and capable of compassion, his beggars often showed a different spirit.

One of his patients in the old 'mules quarters', a young man who could only afford one scanty meal a day and who did not seem to be recovering as quickly as Tom had expected, was found to be sharing the little he had with the man in the next bed, whose employers had first supplied him with food and then abandoned him. Often Tom shared his own food and used precious Mission funds to help those who were penniless. Often, too, there was an old mother in the background, entirely dependent on her sick son's earnings, whom Tom found to be literally starving. One old lady was living on a handful of roast chaff a day.

Sometimes there was no way in which a patient could be accommodated. A young lad who came to Peking looking for work was living on a bowl of *chow* a day and had no means at all of feeding himself in hospital. Tom took him home and Grace looked after him with her own boys till he was cured and able to find work.

For about a month after his family's arrival in Peking, Tom enjoyed a relaxed, almost pastoral, interlude, when he was able to get out of the city and into the countryside. He was able to enjoy observing Chinese modes of life and embark on a new bout of creative activity. Despite the extra demands on his resources, he decided to push on and create new dispensaries and 'hospitals' in outlying districts. His diary reports his spending a good deal of money on erecting wards, and his hope of persuading the people of the district to subscribe money to help defray the running expenses.

In almost discursive style, Tom recorded that on April 8th he had made a journey to Shih Pa Li Tien on the annual 'grave repairing day' when the mounds everywhere were topped with paper money. He had seen a little mud house with three small openings curtained with red cloth, in which a hedgehog was fed and regarded with veneration. '*It is supposed*,' he observed whimsically, '*that its worship ensures wealth to the devotee*.' He also commented on a beautiful white pagoda which was believed to have risen mysteriously overnight some time in the distant past. Tom was almost beginning to like China.

Suddenly this peaceful and expansive time was brought to an end. In late May rumours began to circulate that an epidemic of cholera was on its way. Tom was already treating a poor rat-worshipping family whose father died of cholera. He accepted the offer of a bungalow in the beautiful Western hills for his family to use during the hot months. Peking in high summer was, in any circumstance, no fit place for European boys who had not yet had time to become acclimatised. Peking stank and was utterly filthy. In this crisis, escape from it for the family was doubly acceptable. They went off happily, looking forward to the freedom of a country holiday. Tom did not relish a further separation from his family but by now he was more than uneasy at the situation building up in Peking. He had not dared to make proper investigations into the rumours he had heard for the past two weeks, but the day after Grace's departure with the boys, he was brought face to face with the reality of the scourge now spreading rapidly throughout the city. One of his better-educated and well-to-do patients sought him out at home and told him that the previous day he himself had stood at one of the gates of the city for four hours and had counted eighty coffins being carried through the gate in that time. And that was only one of the many gates to the city.

'Can you not do something, *Taifu*?' he asked anxiously. 'Nobody knows what to do and there is nobody to tell us. This is the worst trouble any of us can remember. I have sent my family away, but there are thousands who cannot leave the city. The dying is terrible and in no time whole families will be wiped out.'

Tom looked at the man and studied his expression. Despite his habitual calm, the man's distress was evident. Here was a Chinaman actually pleading with a hated Westerner with great emotion and earnestness, to do something for his city and his fellow citizens. By that time Tom did not need any pleadings to reinforce his own belief that a disaster of unbelievable dimensions was descending upon Peking. Muddled and contradictory advice issued from the Provincial Government at Tientsin had served only to make the Chinese so confused and afraid that they would not go near a foreign hospital. This same patient told him that a story was going around that foreign doctors were deputed to go about amongst the Chinese and if any Chinaman's face gave an indication of disease, they were to carry him off and throw him into a furnace. Tom's dispensary that day was empty of patients. It was pre-Boxer Chaoyang all over again, he thought. The death-carts were everywhere, picking up corpses as though they were garbage – which, indeed, from a medical point of view, they were – and highly dangerous garbage at that. In the rush to collect and get rid of the bodies, most of the elaborate and expensive ceremonial and obsequies of death and burial were being discarded. Those who handled the cholera-stricken bodies were at great risk themselves, and in burying the dead, they were as likely as not to be dead themselves within a couple of days.

Here was the capital city of a great Empire that knew little or nothing of germs, contamination, hygiene, or sanitation, had no public health laws and no-one to give a lead as to how to deal with an epidemic. '*They are so filthy and ignorant*' Tom wrote plaintively, while he wrestled with the problem of how he, a hated foreigner, could possibly do anything to alleviate the situation.

After two days of ghastly sights and sounds, Tom could stand it no longer. He decided that although he had no authority whatever to speak for, or to, the Chinese, he was morally obliged to do so. He decided to visit Sir Robert Hart. Sir Robert Hart was the Head of the Chinese Customs Service in Peking. He had lived almost fifty years in China, and was one of the very few British officials to be respected and trusted by the Chinese. He had proved himself incorruptible in his work, had never defaulted or failed in his financial obligations to the Chinese and was in consequence a popular figure. His general *bonhommie* and cheerful disposition appealed to the Chinese. He never preached at them or lectured them.

Tom confronted him with his own conviction of the responsibility he felt he ought to take. 'Absolutely no precautions are being taken,' he told Sir Robert, 'and we could cut the death rate in half immediately if only people knew what they ought to do when cholera hits them. As it is, the epidemic will soon spread all over the country.' He thought anxiously of Grace and the boys, not half a day's journey from Peking.

Sir Robert eyed him. 'What do you think should be done?' he asked. He was genuinely fond of the Chinese people and wanted to help.

Tom was ready. 'The Court should issue public instructions – edicts, if necessary – about the precautions that must be taken. I doubt if they know themselves. If I draw up a list of simple precautions, do you think you could get them posted around the city?'

'Right,' said Sir Robert Hart. He liked the young Scottish doctor and found his concern for the Chinese a welcome change from the superior and disdainful attitude shown by most British diplomats towards them, and the disapproving attitude of some of the missionaries. 'I want you to go to the man who I think is enlightened enough and has sufficient authority to deal with this. Wait, I'll give you a note.' He scribbled a few lines of introduction and handed them to Tom. The letter was addressed to Prince Su.

'Have you met him?' he asked the doctor, noting his look of incredulity as he took the note.

'We have – er – met,' said Tom, 'but I have not been properly introduced.'

'Right,' said Sir Robert again. 'Well, now you will be, and I hope he will co-operate.'

Tom left Sir Robert's house with the same odd feeling he had experienced on the day Prince Su had landed at his feet. It was as though a higher power than his own was directing him. All he desired was the good of the Chinese. Was *this* the next step towards the Dragon Throne? He had not as much as suggested a particular individual at Court to whom he could apply for help, nor had Sir Robert any knowledge of his previous encounter.

In Prince Su's presence, the odd feeling left him. The Prince looked at him quizzically as he unfolded the note of introduction. It was obvious he remembered the episode of his runaway cart and was not averse to further encounter with the young doctor. He welcomed Tom with great dignity. There was no hint in this Mongol prince of any patronage or superiority. In all his future dealings with him, Tom found a man of extraordinary charm, intelligence and integrity – a true friend who was the soul of generosity and kindness. He could trace his ancestry back to the very beginning of the *Ch'ing* Dynasty when Mongols were incorporated into the Imperial clan. He readily agreed to Tom's proposals and urged him to return to the Palace as soon as he could, with the notices for posting around the city. 'Thank you for coming,' he said, 'we certainly need your help.'

Walking on air, Tom returned home and within two hours he returned to the Palace and delivered to Prince Su his list of precautions. The following is a literal translation of them –

1. Cholera is at present very prevalent in Peking and we fear it is going to be still more so. If you attend to the following rules the trouble will decrease. If you do not it will increase. This disease is most fatal. Most people who take it die, but if you attend to what follows you will be able to avoid it.
2. What is the origin of cholera? In raw articles of food there are invisible living organisms. Although a thing may look clean, by the use of a microscope you will find myriads of these microbes, e.g. in ice, ice water, unboiled water, raw vegetables and raw fruit. In the vomit and faeces of sick people they are especially numerous.
3. If you want to preserve your life do not eat ice, or anything that has laid directly upon ice; do not drink unboiled water; do not eat raw vegetables or raw fruit. Drink boiled water or tea and eat cooked food and in this way you will escape the disease.
4. In the sick room, whether the man lives or dies, whatever he has soiled by his vomit or faeces, you must destroy by burning. In order to prevent the bedclothes, etc. from being soiled by vomit or faeces, spread grass paper under the patient and when the paper has been soiled, take it and throw it on dry straw and burn

the whole; then disinfect the room by burning sulphur after you have pasted up windows and crevices.
5. Wherever the ground has been soiled by the excreta of the patient, throw lime on it; throw lime into your closets and clean up your courtyards.

With the Imperial seal upon them, these placards were posted by Prince Su at strategic points all around Peking. Immediately there was a rush of bystanders to read them. Those who could not read clamoured for those who could to tell them what they were to do. Although thousands were still to die before the day came when it was certain that the epidemic itself was dead, an abatement of the disease was noticeable shortly after these measures were taken. Mercifully, too, the disease did not spread outside the city. All that had happened was that men, women and children had perished of a vile disease because they were ignorant of simple health procedures and basic laws of hygiene.

Regarding this event, Tom later wrote, '*During the great epidemic of cholera which swept through Peking, I was asked by Prince Su to undertake what was, I think, the first official health campaign on modern lines in China.*' It made him many friends amongst both British and Chinese officials. Sir Robert Hart became a firm friend and Prince Su asked the doctor to attend both him and his son at the Palace.

In future, Tom rode to the Palace, where he knew he would be welcome, in an Imperial cart. The great doors would be thrown open and servants were in attendance to conduct him through the outer courtyards to the intimacy of the Prince's own rooms. There he would sit beside him at sumptuous feasts of many courses, served on silver dishes. He was treated as one of the family.

As likely as not, he would have shared that same day a meagre midday meal with his beggars at the dispensary. What he was to earn in Palace fees he would spend on food for the poor, or on whatever help he could give them.

10

The Empress and the Eunuch

In the months which followed his introduction to the Palace, Tom found himself busier than ever. Not only were his beggars to be looked after, but his 'parish' was now extended to include Palace visits, usually in the evenings. In addition to that, he had opened three separate 'dispensaries' on the outskirts of Peking and building had begun – at last – on the London Mission Hospital itself. Letters were in a constant state of outflow and inflow to and from London, with ceaseless requests for money and yet more money towards the building costs.

'*The plans for the new hospital have just been completed,*' he wrote at the end of 1903, '*and the accommodation aimed at was about thirty beds in the hospital . . . furnishing beds, etc. and equipment would require at least one thousand pounds. We have been compelled to cut our building through the middle, thus erecting about half of it and even the half is going to use up more than I have in hand, leaving furnishing and equipping quite unprovided for. What we are to do I do not know. I can sympathise with the Directors and their financial difficulties, for in my daily work I feel the burden of them. How I wish we could put up our whole building! The site is one of the best in the city, on the street beside the Kettler Memorial.*'

Von Kettler was the German Minister who, when the Boxers were about to attack the Legations, insisted on driving in his sedan chair through the city against all advice, for a conference with the Chinese Board of Foreign Affairs. He was shot at point blank range by his assailant.

As a suitable atonement for this outrage, after the Boxer Rising, the Germans insisted that the Chinese erect a marble memorial to von Kettler. Now, a magnificent archway with three arches, spanned the street. Tom had watched with interest this archway being erected and found it took one hundred and ten horses to move each block of marble. The Germans further insisted that three inscriptions be carved, one over each archway, in three languages – German in the middle, Chinese to one side and Latin to the other. It amused Tom to watch tourists look up at the inscriptions and, being unable to read any of them, turn to their Chinese guide for an explanation. This was always readily given. '*This*,' the guide would say, '*is a monument erected to the memory of the man who killed von Kettler.*'

The hospital's proximity to this rather dubious shrine nevertheless enhanced its prominent position in Peking, and Tom regarded this as an additional benefice.

The poverty in Peking itself weighed him down and he was forced into making charges for medicine and treatment for those who could afford it. '*I am hoping to keep on the premises I occupy now and use them for poorer patients and the beggar class*,' he wrote, '*and when my new hospital is built reserve it for better class patients and for those for whom I can afford hospital clothes. I am much in need of rooms for better class patients. Just this week, one of the most influential men in the Empire came to us to invite our aid in his attempt to give up opium, and for such a case special rooms are a necessity. I am just as much in need of rooms where I can take in some of the utterly destitute people whose condition wrings one's heart. The other day I had to refuse one of these, first, because I had no room for him and second, because I had no money to keep him. He was a beggar lad whose foot was ulcerating off. His father had died and he had not a friend in the world.*' But later, Tom wrote that during the year he had been able to give destitute patients hundreds of free meals and also to supply them with articles of clothing.

Opium addicts seemed to be amongst those most eager to listen to, and receive the Gospel message. One man came from a village about one hundred miles from Peking. He became deeply interested and gave his name in as an 'enquirer'. He returned home where there was no opportunity for further religious instruction, but he wrote two or three times. In his first letter he said how glad and surprised his friends and family had been that he had given up opium. In the next, he invited the hospital evangelist to go to the village and offered to pay for his travelling expenses. He then went on to relate how, in a shop one day, where a man was smoking opium, the old craving had returned to him. '*Then*,' he wrote, '*I saw a vision of a man preaching and exhorting me to trust in Jesus. I resisted the temptation and left the shop.*'

During the year of 1903, there was an increase in the number both of in-patients and out-patients. '*The total number of out-patients amounts to 20,045 and the number of in-patients 243, and this*,' Tom wrote, '*in spite of the fact that during the whole year we have had to continue our work in premises not fit for stables.*'

Another unforgettable feature of the year 1903 was the great drought which seized China. Her people had done all they could to move the gods. In some of the provinces, Tom heard, some people were buying other peoples' children to eat and selling their own to be eaten by strangers. In Peking the contrast between the 'haves' and the 'have-nots' seemed more marked than ever. But by this time Tom was in demand for his services both by the British and the Chinese. As a result of his friendship with Sir Robert Hart, which began during the cholera outbreak of 1902, he had become officially Medical Adviser to the Government. He now had an Imperial cart assigned to him bearing the colours appropriate to his function and status.

In his now frequent visits to the Imperial Palace, Tom had his first insights into both the mystique and the realities of Court life. He had prayed for the ruler of all China and now he was being admitted to the secret fastnesses of the Court and the environment in which she exercised her rule. The Palace itself had an air of mystery about its architectural features, one courtyard opening out endlessly into another. The language of the Court, too, with its frequent allusions to heavenly powers and places, evoked an almost hypnotic descriptive effect. The 'Purple Forbidden City', for instance, was an evocative term introducing a colour sense to add to the strange sights and sounds that a visitor encountered. Visitors, as a matter of fact, rarely did savour these things. Only the highest officials with appointments were admitted, and the servants were confined to the Court. Colours – of clothing, ornaments, flowers, jewels, building materials (including the famous yellow and slate blue tiles) and fabrics – were both subtle and brilliant. The Empire was 'Celestial', the Court was 'Celestial', though its Palace was the most secret in the world and its scandals reeked more of hell than of heaven. The colour almond-yellow was the Imperial colour and most scrolls and official documents were made of yellow watered silk. Imperial sedan chairs were of yellow. Imperial – or 'Sainted' – Commands were written in Vermilion ink. Red was often used for bedroom decoration. Red was also the colour for brides to wear.

The Empress-Dowager's name as a young girl was Orchid, her young sister's Chrysanthemum; the Summer Palace was the 'Round Bright Garden', the Emperor, the 'Lord of Ten Thousand Years', the Great Wall, The 'Purple Barrier', foreigners were 'Red Barbarians'. At death one 'mounted the Dragon and became a Guest on High'.

These colourful and glamorous titles of places and people gave Tom a more romantic view of China than he had hitherto seen in his mud-walled, rat-infested buildings, and to him it became an unfoldment of a fascinating scene largely hidden from the rest of the world.

It also gave Tom renewed interest in the person of the Empress-Dowager herself. He occasionally caught a distant glimpse of her, walking, upheld under both arms by ladies-in-waiting or eunuchs who always accompanied her. But he was not to meet her face to face till the day he was summoned to appear before the Dragon Throne.

In the meantime he came to know the history of her life and career in detail as seen from the Forbidden City or the 'Great Within'; he also picked up, involuntarily, much tittle-tattle about her daily life from eunuch conversation or from the noble and titled ladies who became his patients. The first story he ever heard about her showed her ready wit and ability to defend Chinese customs to the rest of the world. The foreign wife of a Chinese Minister spoke to the Empress-Dowager about foreigners laughing at the custom of Chinese foot-binding. 'What do foreigners use to bind their waists?' she demanded of her questioner and insisted that the latter show her her daughter's stays. She then promptly ordered the daughter a *Manchu* dress. The following day the girl did not appear at Court and on enquiry, the Empress-Dowager was told she was ill. 'I don't wonder,' was her reply, 'it will take her a while to become accustomed to her new clothing after binding herself in steel so that she can hardly breathe.'

The more he thought about the Empress-Dowager the more Tom began to feel some sympathy with her. The *Manchus* themselves were a foreign usurping power and were distinctly unpopular in parts of China. The Throne itself had tottered at the close of the T'ai Ping Rebellion fifty years earlier, and the Empress-Dowager's own position had then been threatened. He could not think of any single benefit that the British as traders or as soldiers had brought to China, and there genuinely was no reason why the Empress-Dowager should have the slightest feeling of benevolence towards them. They had burnt down her splendid and beautiful Palace twice, and during the recent Boxer Rising, the English had joined in the looting and vandalism as much as any other nation. All her life, the Empress had exhibited a remarkable self-survival quality which was almost, if not quite, pathological.

Perhaps this was attributable to the fact that she herself had no claims to Imperial power. She was the daughter of a minor Manchu official and had been picked out to be a Class Three concubine to the late Emperor Tsung-Fien in 1853, by his mother. She was then a girl of sixteen, but right from the beginning she had had designs on the Throne itself. The Emperor was a dissipated man worn out by his own excesses and follies. His Empress, who had been a Class Two Concubine, had borne him a daughter who was weakly and died young. Tzu-Hsi, it was widely rumoured and believed, had caused the Emperor's death by poisoning with the help of his Grand Eunuch. She had previously either borne him a son, or had succeeded in smuggling a baby born of peasant stock into the Palace whom she had passed off as her own. At the Emperor's death, she and the Empress, Tsu-An, became co-Regents, having foiled a plot for their assassination by three elected Regents, whom she outwitted and had executed after divulging their plot publicly. The two women shared the Throne, Shu-An in the East, Tzu-Hsi in the West. Shu-An had now been given the title of Empress-Dowager and Tzu-Hsi herself was given the same title by virtue of having produced an heir. Tsu-An was a weak and rather silly woman, and it was Tzu-Hsi who was *de facto* ruler. She ruled both the Court and the nation with a ruthless determination. The two women would hold audience jointly, sitting on two thrones behind a yellow curtain. Petitioners or Councillors had to kneel on the far side of the curtain and read out their petitions or Memorials in the general direction of the curtain. It was Tzu-Hsi who gave all the answers, the petitioner knowing he was dismissed when the voice stopped.

As her son grew up and neared his coming of age and right to sit on the Dragon Throne, Tzu-Hsi determined she was not going to let her own power slip away. He had refused to marry the woman she had designated for him, whom she could have used as a spy and accomplice, but had married a woman of his own choice. By overhearing a conversation between them in which it was revealed that the Empress-elect was pregnant and that they both intended to claim their rights to the Throne, the Empress-Dowager acted swiftly. Could it be a coincidence that Tung-Chi, her son, was visited by the disease of the 'hundred flowers' (smallpox) or did she, in visiting him, manage somehow to manipulate his illness? Nobody knew for sure, but one thing was certain. He died and the young widow was invited to commit suicide by Tzu-Hsi, who sent her the silken cord with which to do the hanging, together with a note which read, '*Share his joy as well as his sorrow, riches, or poverty and in death be buried with him as in life you shared his guilt.*' The Empress, hitherto irrepressible, did as she was told.

Tzu-Hsi promptly appointed her sister's son, Kuang Hsu, heir to the throne of China – he was only three years old – and was all set for a good long span of rulership. She would have enjoyed it better if the throne had not been divided, though it could not be said that Shu-An was anything more than just a nuisance. However, in 1881, Tzu-Hsi patience wore thin and she despatched her co-Regent a basket of poisoned cakes. Shu-An was rather greedy by nature and ate the lot. The same day Tzu-Hsi found herself ruler of all China. She enjoyed this position so much that she had no intention of relinquishing power to anyone as long as she lived. The young Emperor, Kuang-Hsu, timid by nature, but with an enquiring mind, had grown up at the Court always attended by eunuchs, and quite unused to doing anything for himself. He differed, however, from the Chinese in one respect. As a child he had liked Western toys, and as he grew up his interest in the West had deepened. He began to read Western books, including the New Testament, and as a result was fired with an enthusiasm for change in the centuries-old system of Civil Service examinations founded on Confucianism. He became involved with the Reformers, headed by K'ang Yu-Wei, a reformist scholar. Kuang-Hsu began to issue one edict after another from the Emperor's Palace, proclaiming reforms in the educational system and the Armed Forces. There were to be new schools and colleges, including a University at Peking. He appealed to the people of China by pointing out that the foreign powers surrounded the Empire . . .

and unless the Chinese could learn to adopt the sources of their strength, their plight could not be remedied. Tzu-Hsi became alarmed and appalled at the suggested programme of reform. Kuang-Hsu, meantime, had confided in Yuan Shih-k'ai, a senior Army officer who had distinguished himself as Commander in the Chinese Army. He mistook his man. Kwang-Hsu suggested that troops surround the Empress-Dowager at her Hill of a Myriad Longevities and hold her there. The plot was betrayed to her, and in a terrifying manner she arrived at her nephew's door. He was imprisoned in a four roomed chalet on the edge of the Lake of the Winter Palace. He was forced to abdicate, the Empress-Dowager giving out that he was ill and had requested her to resume the Regency. A new heir-apparent was appointed, again only three years old. From that time, the Emperor lived a life of humiliation, frustration, and helplessness. If present at an Audience at Court in the Palace, he was made to sit on a stool at the feet of his terrible aunt, and whenever summoned into her presence, he had to kneel before her and make profound obeisance.

The version of the life and acts of Tzu-Hsi which Tom acquired at Court stimulated his interest more than ever in the dynastic history and especially the part played by the eunuch system which had demoralised and brought down the previous (*Ming*) Dynasty, and now, he thought, might well do the same to the present *Ch'ing* Dynasty. He was himself becoming more and more involved as medical adviser to these Palace servants and able to observe the problems at very close range.

There were said to be between two and three thousand eunuchs in the Palace and Tom was to treat literally hundreds of them. The most common complaint from which they suffered was one only the surgeon's knife could cure and it was one which Chinese doctors were quite unable to treat.

In addition, they suffered from psychological causes inherent in their condition. '*The physiognomy of a eunuch is peculiar and the trained eye can pick him out at once*,' wrote Tom. '*His temper is peculiar and he is often cruel, as his wife knows to her sorrow.*' Several of his eunuch patients were married, and this tended to exacerbate rather than alleviate their problems.

At the head of all these Palace servants, who acted as butlers, cooks, clerks, hairdressers, messengers and house servants, was the Great Chamberlain, or Grand Eunuch, Li Lien-Ying, also nick-named 'Cobbler's Wax Li', who had been apprenticed to a cobbler in his youth until at the age of sixteen his ambition to attain the post of leading eunuch caused him to castrate himself. This notorious man, who came from Ho Chien in Chihli, from which most of the eunuchs – described by one writer as 'rats and foxes' – had come, had reached a position of unassailable power where his lightest whim was law in the 'Forbidden City'. He had so managed to ingratiate himself with the Empress-Dowager that he was now her favourite above all others. She permitted him unusual liberties, such as remaining seated in her presence, even when she was on the throne itself. In the privacy of her apartments he was allowed to eat with her – a privilege denied to everybody else – and to discuss whatever subjects he chose. He had become her regular and authoritative adviser on important matters of State. Even to high officials, who bitterly resented it, he would often refer to the Empress-Dowager and himself as *tsamen* ('we two'), a familiar phrase implying equality. He called her 'Old Buddha', a corruption of her title as 'Holy Mother'. Most sacrilegious of all he used the title among his followers of 'Lord of Nine Thousand Years' in contradistinction to the Emperor's official title of 'Lord of Ten Thousand Years'. He aped the Emperor's manners and habits in a way to make him appear ridiculous.

He was alleged to be corrupt, avaricious, vindictive and fiercely cruel to his enemies and rivals, but wholly dedicated and faithful to his imperial mistress. Under her protection and with her full knowledge, he organised a system of '*corvées*' (enforced unpaid labour), squeezes, and '*douceurs*' (bribes). A word in the ear of his mistress in favour of an applicant for official position was estimated as worth tens of thousands of pounds to this Palace favourite, whose own apartments were stacked with silks and *objets d'art*. He often shared the proceeds with 'Old Buddha'. He encouraged lavish expenditure, and most scandalous of all, China's humbling defeat at the hands of Japan in 1894 was largely due to his diversion of funds from the Navy to the reconstruction and decoration of the Summer Palace with the Empress-Dowager's connivance. He levied rich tribute on the eighteen provinces of China. He boasted that he could make or mar the highest officials at his pleasure and defy the Son of Heaven on his Throne. '*He wielded a power*' wrote Tom, '*beside which that of the barber in the Court of Louis XI was trivial.*'

At the time of the escape from Peking of the Empress-Dowager and members of her Court in the Boxer Rising, Li Lien Ying was less fortunate than his royal mistress, for he lost the whole of his buried treasure in the capital. It had been '*cached*' in a place known only to his intimate subordinates, but one of these sold the secret to the French troops. He returned penniless. However, within a relatively short time he was reputed to be fabulously wealthy once more and to be worth two million Sterling.

It was said that he hated the young reforming Emperor because the Emperor had once ordered him to be thrashed. Tom felt this story was quite likely to be true, because Kuang Hsu, like all reformers, would have liked to have abolished the eunuch system. Had his abortive attempt to bring in reform been successful, Li Lien Ying's head would have been forfeited. The Grand Eunuch's hatred of the Emperor was an important factor in the estrangement between the Emperor and the Empress-Dowager after the *coup d'état* of 1898, and he played a continuing part in helping to keep the unfortunate Kuang Hsu in a position of submission and helplessness, and to demean him in every way possible. He could not, in the case of the young Emperor, act, as he often did, as the Empress' private executioner, as this murder would be too obvious.

The atmosphere at Court Tom perceived to be always one of intrigue, scandal, and secrecy, giving an almost paralysing sense of insecurity. A hairdresser could be executed for merely making a small mistake in the management of the Empress-Dowager's *coiffure*. In her good moods, she exercised a magnetic charm on everybody who came within her orbit, but Tzu-Hsi in a temper could be terrifying.

In his youth, Li Lien Ying was reputed to have been very handsome. He was still tall and broad-shouldered and had a heavy, powerful body. He, too, could be a formidable and forbidding figure when in a rage.

Tom realised that Li was *the* power behind the Throne and in this situation it would be impossible for him to even 'touch the Throne of China' except through the Empress' favourite. He continued to visit the Palace, sometimes attending eleven-course dinners in private apartments amongst the nobility, sometimes attending eunuchs in their humbler quarters. He never met the Head Eunuch who was nearly always in attendance upon the Empress-Dowager. 'So near and yet so far,' thought Tom, as month after month dragged by, and he was called in yet again for yet another eunuch and his complaints. He prayed for patience in this tantalising situation. The plans for the hospital were going ahead; the plans for the medical training college were in abeyance and must wait.

And then suddenly, one night in the spring of 1904, the night bell in his Chinese house rang, then rang again, imperiously.

Hurriedly, Tom snatched up a dressing gown and hurried to the door. Outside, in the moonlight, stood a tall, solid figure, muffled up in a great surcoat, and behind him a small, insignificant figure in attendance.

'I am in a great hurry,' said Li Lien Ying, 'I can only leave the old Buddha when she is asleep to attend to my own affairs. May I come in?'

11

'Chinese Nicodemus'

Tom's thoughts were chaotic as he conducted the Grand Eunuch across the entrance hall and into the small room he had converted into a 'better-class patients' consulting room. Here there was the luxury of a proper examination couch, an European-type desk and two chairs. Li Lien Ying signalled that he did not wish for his attendant eunuch to accompany him beyond the door, so Tom ushered the timid, small creature into the Cochranes' living room. He was obviously a frightened little man who did not want to be involved in his master's private affairs any more than he had to be. Tom found later that he was afflicted with deafness and also had a speech problem – not a likely threat to any disconcerting revelations within the network of Palace gossip.

As Tom returned to the consulting room, memories of the Grand Eunuch's frightening reputation as a punishing agency of Her Imperial Majesty came to him and the muscles of his stomach tightened. Was he guilty of some reprehensible, if innocent, conduct in his dealings with the Palace patients? Was this visit in the nature of an Imperial warning that he had gone too far in the introduction of Western techniques in the healing craft, or the precursor of an Imperial threat to the future course of his work? He thought of the scores of eunuchs he had been treating and counselling over the past months. This great man, lolling in the patient's chair in front of his desk, had only to whisper a word of malicious criticism into the Empress-Dowager's ear, and Tom's activities and even his life could come to a sudden end. On the other hand, if it were a bribe that Li Lien Ying had in mind, he was certainly going to be disappointed, for Tom was struggling daily with an almost unbearable financial burden.

To Tom's great relief, it was the Grand Eunuch who was suffering some slight embarrassment. After a few preliminaries of polite conversation, he came to the point. He had heard, he said, that Tom had been able to alleviate some of the eunuchs' very specific problems in a way that no Chinese doctor could do. He would like a physical examination himself.

As the doctor turned down the cover on the examination couch, it came to him in a flash that not only his apparently soulless hard work amongst the Palace population over the last year was now bearing fruit, but that his prayer on top of the pile of rubble some three years ago was about to be answered. The Grand Eunuch was visiting him, secretly, by night, not to reprimand him nor seek to stifle his endeavours, but to ask for his help. There was no doubt truth in his saying that he was unable to leave the 'Old Buddha' to attend to his own affairs except when she was asleep, but that did not mean that she was not in his confidence and he in hers, even over the most intimate affairs. Tom had no doubt that Li Lien Ying had come to him at her behest and that she knew all that went on in the Palace.

As Tom gently explained what had to be done and how the effects would need to be treated over a period of time, involving further visits on the Grand Eunuch's part, he marvelled at this Nicodemus-like situation at dead of night. Could anyone but his God have brought about a meeting such as this, of confidences given at the level of deepest need, with no prying eyes, nobody within earshot, nobody to interrupt and nobody to report the details of their conversation? Could he possibly use this opportunity, as his Lord had done with the real Nicodemus, to bring some light to this powerful man with all the distortions of his body and mind? He would need to go gently – one tactless slip of the tongue, a single inference of criticism, and Li Lien Ying would never set foot in his house again. Tom could not afford to tell this man that he needed to be born again. He could not afford to lose this patient, either. All he could do was try to impart a little of the truth to him as they went along.

Half an hour later, when Tom had lowered the big man back into his chair, had told him to rest while he made tea for them both in the kitchen and returned with a tray, the Grand Eunuch appeared mild, good-tempered and jolly. As his huge frame relaxed, he began cheerfully describing his Palace duties and chatted, apparently light-heartedly though always with deep respect, about his Imperial mistress's whims and fancies. Tom ruminated inwardly that a doctor usually sees both the best and the worst of his patients. He could discern no 'worst', nor detect the slightest sinister trait in Li Lien Ying's conversation. Tom never was to see 'the worst' as his doctor.

It was hard to believe that this man, now so much at ease and talking quite freely about himself, this one-time cobbler's apprentice, was one and the same as the great Chamberlain who had stage-managed the poisoning of the old and grey and foolish Tzu-An and was prepared and ready to declare Tzu-Hsi's assumption as sole ruler at the exact moment of her co-regent's death, had enforced the drowning of the Emperor's favourite and much-loved Pearl Concubine in the Palace well as the Empress-Dowager and the Emperor were forced to flee Peking and now was a constant menace to the young Emperor's life and interests.

It was odd, thought Tom, that though he had made a fixed resolve before he left his own country to come as a missionary to China, never to put men's bodies before their souls and never to use his medical skills primarily as a means to evangelising, yet in practice it always seemed to work out that the Achilles' heel of people who might otherwise be his opponents proved to be some weakness of the flesh for which their own philosophy or religion or experience made no provision. And it was only through this breach that he could reach any of them. The poor Mongols had accepted him because he alleviated their pain and cured their diseases, and to some extent shared their hardships. The liberal-minded philanthropic Chinese, like Prince Su (though he also was a Mongol) were drawn to him because he knew how to save lives and put a stop to medical disasters occurring to large numbers of people. Even Peking-born Chinese doctors were beginning to come to him. One had come to him recently, imploring his aid for his son whom he could not cure. 'He is my son,' he cried to Tom, 'my only son.' Now, it seemed, eunuchs were beginning to love him because he understood the nature of their physical troubles and how to give them relief. Where did souls come into it all?

As the two men talked, Tom himself began to relax and to unfold to the great man some of his sorrows in Mongolia and his efforts to relieve physical distress and poverty. The Boxer Rising, for which Li Lien Ying had been held to be the chief instigator, was never mentioned. Tom told him of the nomads, the lamas, the desperately poor city dwellers with roofless houses and the prisoners condemned to execution. He told him of the many patients who had come long distances to see him but had arrived too late for any treatment to be possible, but also of the many on whom he had operated and received back their sight. On the spur of the moment, Tom found himself confiding his great and secret ambition to train young Chinese in Western medicine, as he had trained Lui-i in Chaoyang. He told Li Lien Ying how it felt to be the only doctor in thousands of square miles of territory, seeing and being unable to cure so many afflictions which could be totally avoided if only there were sufficient qualified Chinese to deal with them, and to teach the people the elements of good health. He described, finally, to Li Lien Ying the fearful problems of the homeless beggars he had since found in Peking and his efforts to convert disused stables into hospital wards.

As they talked, the Grand Eunuch leaned forward, planted both elbows on the desk and stared fixedly at Tom as he talked. That he knew of Prince Su's patronage of the doctor and his work at the Palace, there was no doubt, since it was these things which had prompted his own visit. But apparently he had had no knowledge nor appreciation of Tom's years in Mongolia, nor of his present efforts to help the beggars in Peking. It became clear to him that Tom had spared himself no effort in learning the Chinese language and that he was prepared, if a college were to be set up for Chinese students, to train them in Mandarin Chinese. What more could be desired or asked of a foreigner who was so much in love with his host country that he was prepared to share his skills and knowledge with the Chinese in their own language? Tom was certainly unusual and different from other foreigners he had met. Tom impressed him. Possibly his description of the sufferings of the poor touched some spark of remembrance of his own humble and sordid origins, from which he had taken such drastic steps to escape. He gave no sign to this effect, but he remained talking to Tom till well on into the night and when he left, Li Lien left thoughtfully, having made an appointment to return the following week for further treatment. He also had agreed to meet Dr Li Hsiao Ch'un, Tom's Chinese colleague from the old London Missionary Society Hospital.

Within a day Tom received from the Imperial Palace a beautiful little porcelain flower pot, with a rare plant in it. With it was a note inscribed with the Chinese ideogram meaning, 'With friendship'.

When he met Dr Li Hsiao Ch'un the following day at his dispensary south of the city and described the Grand Eunuch's visit, the Chinese doctor's face lit up. He grasped Tom's coat lapels and almost shook him in his excitement.

'Do you realise what this means, *Taifu*?' he exclaimed. 'Do you realise? The next thing he will do will be to tell you to petition the Throne to build your college and then he will back you up. You must be ready, *Taifu*, for whatever he suggests.'

Tom's innate Scottish caution surfaced. He tried to calm the other man down. 'Not so fast, Li,' he said, 'not so fast. He has not suggested anything for me to do yet. Let us wait patiently and see how he gets on with his own treatment.'

Li refused to be put down. 'Then I will come to your house for his next appointment, *Taifu* – that is, if you agree. I know Li Lien Ying's ways. When he is persuaded, then he will do all that he can – and that,' he added expressively, 'is *everything*! He is the only one the "Old Buddha" really listens to and she never refuses him anything.'

Tom did not reply. He was busy with his own thoughts – second thoughts. Could it really be God's doing that his prayer to 'touch the Throne of China' should be answered in such a bizarre fashion? That the man who had not only encouraged the Boxer Rising but had goaded the Empress-Dowager to give it her support and thereby was responsible for the murder of hundreds of missionaries – many of them doctors – should now be the instrument for a complete reversal of this policy? Would he rehabilitate those whom he had previously persecuted, to the point of giving them positions of authority and teaching? Would it even be right for him, Tom, to accept such help? – or was such help irreversibly tainted?

Li seemed to pick up his thoughts. 'Don't forget, *Taifu*,' he argued, 'that you have done nothing of yourself to bring this about and if the Lord wants to use the heathen or the wicked to fulfil his purposes, who are we to refuse him? You did not pray to meet Prince Su; you did not make the cholera epidemic happen; you did not ask to treat the Palace eunuchs. They have all been brought to you. You did not ask, either, to meet Li Lien Ying. *No*!' he added emphatically, 'it is all the Lord's doing, and it is marvellous in our eyes. Cannot you see it that way, *Taifu*?'

Reluctantly, Tom had to agree. He knew that the ultimate motivation of his prayer to touch the Dragon Throne had been an unselfish one. He had simply wanted to help China in its ignorance and its need. In treating Li Lien Ying, he had not breached any moral or aesthetic law and in one way he felt deep compassion for the man. Where would he be without his beloved mistress and patroness? Not for the first time in his life, Tom thanked God that his own ultimate trust was in him and not in any human affection or devotion, although he gave and received plenty of this in his family. He thought back to his early days in Greenock, the constant shadow of poverty stalking him at every turn, the premature burden of family responsibility placed upon him by his father's death, the enormous efforts and work he had put into becoming qualified as a doctor, all with the further aim to serve God in whatever part of the world he chose to put him. And God had sent him to China – he was sure of that.

Li Lien Ying, too, had had a hard struggle, but in a totally different environment, and he had longed for an escape into a fuller and more rewarding life. He had not had the benefit, as Tom had, of being introduced to Jesus and there had been nothing in Chinese life or religion, or in his eunuch-orientated background, to inspire him spiritually to serve and love and help his fellow men. He had paid the highest penalty possible in the sacrifice of his manhood at an early age, to attain his worldly ideal. He had undoubtedly laid up earthly treasure for himself and power over others, but what would be the outcome of it all? He had no family and no true friends. It was all a question of values, thought Tom, remembering his own thirteenth birthday vow to be 'God's forever, with his help.'

He could not and would not judge Li Lien Ying, and if God permitted some acts of grace to happen through him, then it was surely a matter for praise and not for questioning. But he still permitted himself to wonder what exactly *had* changed the Grand Eunuch's outlook.

The two men met at Tom's house at the time of Li Lien Ying's next appointment. A benign, jovial Grand Eunuch arrived, his tiny attendant trotting behind him, about midnight. He was more reserved in his manner with the Chinese doctor than he was with Tom, which surprised the latter; but he listened attentatively to all that Dr Li had to say. He took for granted that Tom still wanted to pursue his plan and as Dr Li Tsaio Ch'un had forecast, his advice was, 'Petition the Throne! Do it at once and I will advise her Majesty to give her approval!'

'All very well,' Tom thought, 'but what am I going to ask of her?' The urgent need was for money but he could hardly present such a bold, bald material petition without forewarning. It would not be in accordance with Chinese *étiquette* and besides, he needed to give the Empress convincing evidence or proof of his own motives and intentions on behalf of the Chinese people.

For the second time since his arrival in Peking, he walked right round the walls of the 'North City' (which enclosed the 'Forbidden City' and the 'Imperial City'), praying at every step. He also visited his 'Bethel' stone out on the Western hills. Finally, he decided to consult his patient and friend at Court, the Grand Councillor, Na T'ung. Apart from Li Lien Ying, Na T'ung was the closest of the Chinese ministers to the Manchu Empress and he was, if not a wholly committed Christian, very much in sympathy with Tom's aims and work. Tom prayed earnestly that Na T'ung would advise him correctly and he drove to his Palace to visit him. To his amazement, Na T'ung seemed so pleased to see him that he even embraced him – a very unusual gesture for a Chinese – and immediately begged Tom to go and see his mother who was seriously ill. She was in her eighties and Na T'ung was quite certain that she would not recover. 'All the same,' he said to Tom, 'you have come in time, perhaps in the nick of time.' He had been to all the Legations that morning, he told Tom, saying that his mother was on her deathbed and that he would have to retire for the long period of mourning appropriate to such a bereavement.

Without Tom saying a word about his own request, he hurried off to see the old lady, gave her the necessary treatment and determined to pray again for her recovery. He returned to Na T'ung, told him what he had done and the arrangements he had made for her care and his intention to continue to pray for her recovery. Having reassured Na T'ung as far as possible, he then recounted to him the Grand Eunuch's advice. Na T'ung immediately promised that he would not only word Tom's petition appropriately, but that he himself would present it to the Empress, irrespective of the outcome of his mother's illness.

Tom went out once more to the Western hills and knelt by his 'Bethel' stone. There he prayed the dual prayer – for the old lady's recovery and for the success of his petition. The spot he had selected was one which had been chosen by an emperor of earlier times, who had written the following lines –

'Why have I scaled this dizzy height,
Why sought this mountain den?
I tread as on enchanted ground
Unlike the abodes of men.
Weird voices in the trees I hear,
Weird visions see in air;
The whispering pines are living harps,
And fairy hands are there.
Beneath my feet my realm I see
As in a map unrolled,
Above my head a canopy
Bedecked with clouds of gold.'

As he rose from his knees and gazed down on the city of Peking, Tom felt the same divine peace flowing into him as he had experienced when he had prayed in that same spot for China as a nation to be won for Christ. To him it was as if the prayer were already answered.

To everyone's astonishment, the old lady recovered and this strengthened Tom's faith in the coming answer to his greater petition. On a day he would never forget, news came through to him from official circles that the Empress-Dowager had donated ten thousand ounces of silver in response to his petition for help to build the medical college.

'*Such a unique gift,*' Tom wrote, '*the first of its kind in the history of China, made front page news. Dr Morrison, who was* The Times *correspondent in Peking, came round to see me for confirmation of this news before cabling the news to London.*'

Within twenty-four hours, the front page of every Western national newspaper carried the startling statement that the Empress-Dowager of China had given, not only a large sum of money, but also her official patronage and approval to the first-ever Medical Training College for Chinese students to be founded in China, to be staffed by foreign missionaries whom five years earlier she would willingly have had executed.

12

The Duchess Kotows

Tom had been amazed on his arrival in Peking to find that the different denominational Protestant missionary societies, both European and American, who were beginning to send their men back into China after the signing of the Peace Treaty, all operated independently of one another and made no attempt at co-operation. All bore names relevant only to the supporting denominations in their homelands. None of these names meant anything to the Chinese and the only effect of this exclusiveness and division was to confuse them.

Why were there so many groups of foreign people who claimed to have the same beliefs, yet ignored each other, or at least did not seem to want to know each other, if they were so keen to turn the Chinese into Christians? Which was the real, true church? It was a puzzle to the Chinese and it was a pain to Tom. His previous work in Mongolia had been of such a pioneering and lonely nature that he could not understand how devoted, dedicated Christians, whose aims were presumably the same as his own, could possibly be blind to the great opportunity now being offered to them. As far as his Mission was concerned, he had been put in charge of no less a job than to re-organise and co-ordinate the whole of the educational work for North China. He himself was loyal to the London Missionary Society, but saw no reason why that loyalty should be diminished or spoiled by working in harmony and unity with other missionary societies, or why they should not all pool their resources. He saw with a blinding clarity what a stumbling-block lack of friendship or any sort of spiritual rivalry between 'competing' foreign missionaries could prove to be to the logically minded Chinese. He was aware, too, how closely every foreign effort and attitude was being monitored by Chinese observers. '*By their deeds shall ye know them*,' he wrote in his diary, including himself in this judgment.

From the time when he began his work in the white-washed stables and converted grainshop, this lack of communication between others who had come to Peking with the same desire to bring Christ to China, nagged at him day in and day out. Within a few weeks he was addressing a specially called meeting of the Peking Missionary Association, and reading a paper in which he made the suggestion that, throughout China, a common name should be adopted for churches and chapels. All foreign names and titles (foreign insofar as the Chinese were concerned) should be dropped and each church or chapel should be known only by the name of the locality in which it was situated. 'We must preach,' he said,' not a sectarian Christianity, not the narrow conception of a particular church, but the broad idea of the Kingdom of our Father.' The aim should be to have just one Church of Christ in China. He further suggested that a Committee be formed on Church Union. Tom did not meet much response at this first meeting and no great enthusiasm was shown, but gradually a Committee did come into being, known simply as the 'Union Committee.'

He also foresaw and impressed upon his colleagues that as time went by, they as pioneers would be supplanted by fully trained Chinese doctors, who even if they were not Christians, at least could inherit the spirit in which medical work had been initiated. He emphasised that standards of work and study must attain the highest possible level, to establish a pattern for those who would follow on. He warned of results if this principle were not adhered to.

'*China wants our education, our secrets of applied science, but what if in giving up these secrets, we destroy the ethic which has influenced China for three thousand years and did not give in its place . . . an ethic purer than that of Confucius? Give China the science without the Christianity*,' he said, '*and woe betide us.* We should have raised up a dragon of portentous size and strength, a competitor without scruple or conscience; *and woe to the rest of mankind.*'

By the time his prayer to touch the Throne was realised, a strong union of four different missionary societies had been formed to support and carry out the work of higher education in North China, to which a fifth was added later. When the founding of a medical college turned from a dream into a reality, it was to be known as the 'Peking Union Medical College' – or PUMC as it was known familiarly to the doctors, students and nurses who claimed it as their *alma mater* for years to come. As the London Missionary Society's representative, Tom was the Head of the entire Medical Department of the Union. Other departments set up colleges of Arts, Science and Theology in Peking.

When the news of the Empress-Dowager's patronage and gift came, it spread like wildfire through the Chinese corridors of power, amongst the bureaucrats and mandarinates all over the country, and to every Christian missionary in the whole of China.

At the Imperial Court, a group of high officials formed a small committee, and a subscription book bound in beautiful Imperial yellow silk, with the Empress-Dowager's signature and the amount of her donation at the head, was circulated both within the Court – to princes, dukes, nobles and grand councillors – and then to all Provincial Governors. It was *de rigeur* to follow suit, and with the Imperial example before their eyes, subscriptions were never refused.

There was now no need for delay in getting on with the building of the hospital which Tom had lamented earlier had had to be cut through the middle. Plans were revised to add the college building onto the existing site and only one thing could hold up or spoil the plan. Sitting squarely on the site and fronting right onto the street was a small Government *yamen* which had been located there for a very long time and was in daily use. It was found that this building would spoil the symmetry of the hospital and college. It would also hide that wing of the new building to which the Empress-Dowager's gift had been chiefly allocated. Tom promptly 'memorialised' the Throne again and because it was unthinkable that her Majesty's gift should be obstructed by another building, the *yamen* was promptly dismantled by Imperial decree and a further gift of that portion of land on which it had stood was generously donated, enabling additional college rooms to be built on, facing the street.

The hospital itself was opened before the college building was finished and before long, Tom had a distinguished patient on his hands. This was the Duchess Te, a niece of the Empress-Dowager and one of her favourite ladies-in-waiting. This royal *Manchu* lady moved into the hospital with a bevy of ladies-in-waiting of her own in attendance on her. The Duchess had heard of Tom's skill as a surgeon and was very anxious to have a difficult and delicate operation performed. She was quite willing to come into hospital to have it done. For this special event, Tom was largely dependent on his wife's co-operation in the successful entertainment of such a high *Manchu* lady as a hospital patient.

Grace, however, found herself in an embarrassing and unprecedented situation when she first entered the room which had been set apart for the Duchess' accommodation. Suddenly, all the ladies-in-waiting were commanded to kotow to Grace, which meant knocking their foreheads three times on the floor as they knelt. Even the Duchess prostrated herself. A flustered Grace, her usual self-effacement deserting her, was astonished to find herself the centre of a circle of prostrating *Manchus* and tried to get them back on to their feet. The Duchess, however, continued with her prostrations, calling Grace repeatedly her 'sister'. It appeared that she had developed qualms on entering the hospital and was very much afraid that when she returned to Court, she would get into trouble for allowing a man to operate on her. Throughout this little ceremony, she claimed Grace as her 'sister' and Tom as her 'brother-in-law' and thereafter always referred to them in this way.

On her return to the Palace, she was sent for by the Empress-Dowager, who by then was seething with curiosity to know about the famous, foreign 'sleeping medicine'. She wanted to know all the details of the operation and enquired if it were true that one could have one's body cut open and sewn up again and not be aware of it. She was so intrigued that she commanded the Duchess to have a photograph taken of herself and the doctor – she in *Manchu* clothing and wearing the high *Manchu* headdress, he in morning dress – standing by a little bamboo table in a 'tea ceremony'. This, so far as the Empress-Dowager and the Duchess herself were concerned, sealed the relationship officially. She was also commanded to send the doctor presents and to make a handsome donation to the hospital. But Grace could never get over the fact that she was now a member of the Imperial family.

This incident started off a round of further donations and in due course the Grand Councillor Na T'ung, in conjunction with his daughter and his now fully recovered mother, raised a fund to assist permanently in the running costs of the hospital.

Most of the organisational and fund-raising work had fallen on Tom and in addition to his beggar and palace work, he was now lecturing twice weekly to medical students at the Methodist University. It was then he came up against the problem of the lack of Chinese textbooks. He began, late at night, to do translation work and in two years' time he would be translating Heath's *Anatomy* and Heath's *Osteology* into Mandarin Chinese, for the use of his own college students – a combination of one of the most difficult languages and subjects in the world. He was frequently pushed into inventing ideograms for medical terms for which no Chinese equivalent existed. He found great pleasure and satisfaction in this and his new words became incorporated into the body of medical Chinese terminology. Following Tom's lead, other colleagues made other translations. In the years 1910–11 a Translation Department was to be set up in the college and several of the medical staff were to translate textbooks on surgery, medical jurisprudence, toxicology and physiology.

In considering the medical curriculum for the training of Chinese students, it was necessary to evaluate the current knowledge and methods of the Chinese, who were not without their centuries old practices and traditions. Mostly these consisted of herbal remedies, and the practice of medicine was apt to be in the hands of families in which the medical profession was hereditary. The practitioner was subject to no legal requirements and could practice as he pleased. Patients of Chinese doctors were commonly warned not to put themselves into the care of any doctor whose family had not been practicing medicine for at least three generations.

Prescriptions were like recipes, favourite remedies being carefully guarded secrets, like a chef's favourite dish. There was no scientific knowledge involved; nearly all these remedies were herbal ones passed down as part of a folklore and made up of many ingredients. Chinese medicine could be termed an art rather than a science. Tom found that many of these herbal remedies were efficacious.

Chinese drugstores provided the remedies in abundance. But the making up of prescriptions was a rather hazy procedure. Chemists were not concerned about exact proportions or amounts and patients were seldom advised about dosage. This was largely left to their own discretion.

There was no collected body of knowledge on anatomy or physiology as understood by Western doctors trained in the modern scientific method of the day. The study of the human body, its make-up and functions, was hopelessly frustrated by the traditions of ancestor worship. The very idea of dissection of a body was sacrilegious and its commission would be a crime. The Chinese regarded the whole matter with peculiar horror. Tom puzzled deeply as to how these subjects could be taught to the Chinese, who used ivory manikins with removable lids for diagnosis which, when lifted, revealed weird arrangements of internal organs which could be very confusing. The contents of the abdomen in the figurines shown to Tom by friendly Chinese doctors never seemed to approximate to anything he knew and frequently included organs which did not exist. One chart on record showed the oesophagus as passing through the heart and from there to the liver and from there to the stomach! He felt that, relatively speaking, these sophisticated Peking medical aids to diagnosis were not much improvement on the 'pain in the east of the stomach' descriptions which he had become accustomed to in Chaoyang. Diagnosis was in the main based upon the pulse and Chinese treatises claimed no less than ninety-eight of these in the human body.

The Chinese had absolutely no knowledge or skill in surgery and rarely attempted it. There was the famous story of the man who was accidentally shot by an arrow which lodged in his body. He went to one Chinese doctor, who claimed some skill in surgery, who sawed off the protruding part of the arrow, leaving the remainder embedded. He then recommended the patient to go to a doctor of 'internal medicine' for further treatment, saying he had fulfilled his obligations in the matter.

Tom felt that this lack was the greatest of all lacks in the field of medical education. When he remembered the hundreds of cases of simple cataract operations he had performed in Mongolia and then in Peking, where he was now doing quite advanced surgery, it troubled him greatly to think of the thousands who were sightless but who need not be, not to mention many other conditions which were curable by surgical means only. He and his colleagues would have to do their best to teach without the aid of corpses until the prohibitions of the law could be relaxed, relying on charts, plates and drawings.

About this time, Tom had an unexpected visit from his young assistant, Liu-i, of Chaoyang days. He had travelled down from Mongolia and they met one evening under a full moon, beneath the lime trees in Tom's garden. The meeting between the two men was full of love and in Liu-i's case, fervently expressed emotion.

He had heard of the doctor's success in his Petition to the Throne and the designs for the new College and he was eager to be enrolled as one of the first students when the College opened. As they talked, Liu-i clasped the doctor's hands and with tears repeated his gratitude for all the personal teaching and care he had received from him. His great ambition now was to be able to return to Chaoyang as a fully trained doctor and surgeon, capable of carrying on Tom's previous work so violently disrupted by the Boxer Rising. It was obvious from his account of things that he had done his noble best to continue to treat the hundreds of people who were bereft of their *Taifu* and had no-one else to turn to. Tom regarded this meeting, in later life, as one of the sweetest experiences of his whole lifetime, and when Liu-i brought messages to him from old patients – those to whom he had restored sight or had cured of some pestilential disease, his own eyes filled with tears. He had, in the past, regarded Liu-i almost as a son to him, and he promised to do everything he could to enrol him and make sure that he received the further medical education he needed. The thought that he was not forgotten and that Chaoyang would eventually have a Chinese doctor capable of handling almost anything single-handed, as he himself had done, warmed and comforted him (Liu-i's name appears in the list of first graduating students receiving the Diploma of the College at the hands of the Imperial Board of Education, in the Union Medical College's Report for 1910–11).

By this time, Tom held the posts of Acting Consultant to various Legations, Acting Physician to the British Legation, Medical Officer to the Imperial Maritime Customs and Medical Adviser to the Chinese Government. Once the Empress-Dowager had made her announcement, all doors were open to him and he was as welcome to members of the Royal family as he was to the filthiest and poorest of his original 'family' of Peking beggars. Friends in England were not backward in sending contributions of money and good wishes and throughout the rest of the year 1905, life was an unending and uninterrupted bustle to get ready for the grand 'Opening Ceremony' of the PUMC, to which Tom had petitioned the Empress-Dowager to send her own representative. He himself was to be Principal of the College and hold the Chair of Anatomy, and was already Senior Surgeon to the Hospital.

In the midst of this invigorating and happy time, and forgetting neither his beggars, nor his eunuchs, nor his nobles, Tom made time to found a school of language in Peking specifically to help new missionaries to learn the language on arrival. This school eventually blossomed into the famous Peking Language School.

In the meantime, all was hard work on the college site as workmen installed central heating and a hot water system, put in as modern a sewerage system as possible, and laid the last of the tiles on roof and floors. The Opening Ceremony was fixed for the 13th of March, 1906. The Board of Education had promised to recognise the degrees to be conferred at the end of the training course. Various other Boards promised and gave financial support. All high Chinese officials and every Minister of each of the foreign powers were to be invited to the ceremony.

It is as well that this brilliant occasion was to be fully and widely reported. Modern China appears to have forgotten, or possibly to be ignorant of, that day in China's history when she opened the doors – in a magnificent ceremony in her capital city – of the nation's first-ever medical Training College in the glorious spring of 1906.

13

The Opening

It is difficult to know what Tom's thoughts and feelings were in the backwash of the enormous wave of interest and enthusiasm which broke over Peking after the Imperial announcement of patronage and donation to the proposed new Training College for Chinese students. There appears to have been some sort of crisis of health in his family at just about the same time.

The last entry in his personal diary for 1905 was on 29th December, when he was obviously not in very good health himself and may have been temporarily overwhelmed by events. He prays for an improvement of health and goes on, '*Help me to prepare and deliver sermons in Chinese. Help me to make the spiritual part of the College work a success. Help me to make the College the best in China, the Hospital the best in Peking, and oh, help me, above all, to hasten the time . . .*' The rest of the sentence is lost, as the next few pages of the diary are missing and it remains guesswork as to what he wished to hasten, or what spiritual or mental ordeal he was subjected to in the early months of 1906.

There are no further entries till July of that year when a burst of relief, praise and thanksgiving suggest that he had come through some time of testing and it appears he was absent from Peking for a short time. It may be that the answer to his greatest prayer, even though it had come through a series of well spaced-out events, had been a momentary shock to Tom Cochrane when he fully realised the enormous and far-reaching results which would ensue from the Empress-Dowager's permission and patronage of his treasured scheme. It is certain that he was grossly overworked and was greatly concerned for the preservation of his early morning 'hour', He may have feared that material things were a threat to his spiritual life. Then, was he adequately prepared? Were his colleagues in the Union prepared? Could they really undertake to teach and train the young Chinese so as to turn out, in five years' time, a batch of young doctors fully equipped to deal with all the medical needs and diseases of China?

It was the teaching of surgery which mainly worried Tom. The embargo on the use of human bodies for dissection was a major handicap for him, seeing that he was to hold the Chair of Anatomy and was already Senior Surgeon in the Hospital. Strangely enough, there was little opposition, even amongst the Chinese diehards, to the introduction of Western medicine. Western medicine, but in particular, surgery, was regarded with respect in cities such as Peking, although in country districts many of the old ideas of missionaries performing atrocities, eyes being cut up for medicine, etc., still lingered.

The other worry was the lack of any systematic scheme for the running costs of either Institute. Fees for medical students would, of course, be charged and it was hoped that the College would be self-supporting. Salaries of medical staff were paid by their respective Missions and it had been unanimously agreed that all fees earned privately by medical staff would be paid into hospital funds. Lecturers from outside Peking – who would, of course, be foreign medical missionaries – would give their services free. Fees for the better-class Chinese in-patients of the hospital were already being charged, as also were medicines. Even so, the poor outnumbered the rich in every department of their work. Tom fell back on the fact that the whole scheme had been a venture of faith from the outset and it was not possible at this stage to cross all the 't's or dot all the 'i's. He was certain that he was in God's will for him in China and he did not hesitate to pray and ask for material wants as well as spiritual graces. On the same page of his diary he wrote, '*I want to be right with Thee, my Father, from centre to circumference, in money matters, in time for devotion and family affairs, in studies and the spending of my time*,' and a little lower down, '*I would like to be a millionaire, my Father, for Thy work. Oh, give me money*!'

The morning of March 13th, 1906, dawned bright and beautiful. Spring came early that year in Peking. The sky was a clear, pale, eggshell blue, unflecked by cloud. It was not yet warm enough for the Chinese gentry to discard their furs, but this merely added magnificence and lustre to the pageantry about to take place.

There were barricades all the way through the streets of Peking from the Gate of Heavenly Peace, which guarded the southern approaches to the Imperial Palace, to Hatamen Street, where the Kettler Memorial arched over the street and beyond which stood the much talked of new Hospital and College.

As the Imperial cavalcade emerged from the Imperial City, it seemed as if the whole of Peking had turned out to see this spectacle. Every beggar, even if he were blind and had to be led, was present. Nothing on this scale had ever been staged before in the whole of the city's history. The soldiery had a tough job in keeping the crowds back, but the crowds, ragged and barefoot as most of them were, were eager and in good humour and regarded the day as a national holiday. All the usual vendors were there, the tea-makers, the hot water merchants, the roasted chestnut sellers, the vegetable carters. The booths and tents of fortune-tellers, cobblers, barbers and all the people engaged in the multifarious activities normally carried on in the streets of Peking were busy and crowded.

First in the procession from the Palace came the princes and dukes of the Imperial House, in their red-banded chairs, preceded by outriders on horseback, with a retinue beside and behind. Then came the high officials. Palanquins, carts and rickshaws followed, in what seemed an endless flow, of Foreign Ministers, diplomatic and notable foreigners and their wives. Everybody who was anybody came to this pageant of splendour in old Peking. It was a pleasurable occasion and those who were invited crowded into the large new building, right in the centre of the city.

The Empress-Dowager's own choice of representative was His Excellency N'a T'ung. Apart from his being a member of her Inner Council of the Empire, no doubt she considered him the most appropriate of her ministers to send. She knew not only of the Duchess Te's experience at the hospital but also of the healing of N'a T'ung's aged mother. He had played a big part in the run-up to the building and establishment of the College. He was dressed in full Court dress with lavish furs and allowed himself to be photographed after the Opening Ceremony sitting in a group of Chinese and Western notables, between the British and the American Ambassadors. Sir Robert Hart was also in the front row, as was his opposite number, Prince Su, titular Head of the Imperial Chinese Customs and Maritime Services.

As the swarm of guests poured through the tiled reception hall of the College and into the lecture rooms used for the occasion, they passed some osteological specimens in glass cases, laid out fearfully by Tom Cochrane, who wondered if this would be considered an outrage. '*I was afraid that some of our visitors might think that the bones were those of hospital patients specially done to death in the interests of foreign science.*' A reporter for the LMS *Chronicle*, wrote that this was '*A sight quite sufficient to cause a riot in many provincial towns of China*' at that time. Fortunately, nothing of the kind happened.

The first of the speeches was made by His Excellency N'a T'ung, the Imperial delegate, who announced that he had come to represent the Throne on this occasion and that he was speaking by command of Her Majesty. He spoke in Chinese and went on to say that 'Her Majesty the Empress-Dowager, who has manifested her interest in this College by graciously granting a sum of money towards a foundation, appreciates highly the efforts of all those who have been concerned in the establishment of this most useful and much-needed institution . . . The College was planned by Dr Thomas Cochrane, a gentleman eminent in his profession, who spared no pains in carrying through his project to a successful issue. The result is this well-appointed and modern college, the opening of which we are gathered here to celebrate.'

'That the doctor has been able to achieve this gratifying result is due in a great measure to the hearty co-operation accorded him by Sir Ernest Satow and Sir Robert Hart, the Inspector General of the Imperial Customs. His Excellency the Tartar-General of Mukden and many other prominent Chinese officials helped him with contributions; it is certainly a matter of congratulation that in so short a space of time we should see this substantial building erected and ready to be opened and begin its career of usefulness, and it is my sincere hope that the College will prosper continually, and in the course of time, through the agency of its Faculty and graduates, become an instrument of incalculable benefit to the Chinese and its fame spread far and wide throughout the length and breadth of this Empire of China.'

The next of the speeches was by Sir Ernest Satow, Minister of Health to Peking, who spoke of the honour he had in knowing Dr Lockhart who had come to Peking, friendless and unknown, in

1861, and started the work of the old Hospital. He explained that they had met to inaugurate a new medical college and hospital in Peking on a larger scale, and with a more complete staff of professors and general equipment than had ever been attempted hitherto.

Sir Robert Hart followed him. He also had had the pleasure of the acquaintance of Dr Lockhart. 'His was the prophetic vision that saw how medical learning would one day find a field and home and a welcome in China.' Sir Robert referred to the great work which this college would certainly accomplish in future years. Some of the students would be unusually receptive and inventive and would make new revelations in medical science which would benefit the world. Men would no longer need to go abroad for a medical education. Sir Robert pointed out the coming need for a medical department in the Chinese Army, and thought that it was only a matter of time for the Institution to receive regular Government support. No country valued education more than China. She had not yet embarked upon supporting educational institutions as had other countries, but the time had come for her to do so. He went on, 'The fine college is now complete and largely equipped, but the question of its support is at the present time a serious one and falls as a heavy burden upon the shoulders of those who have worked so unwearingly for the various services. In the meantime, however, those who are interested in medical research in new lands, and those who desire to see a Christian spirit guiding the new aspirations towards reform in this land, could hardly use their gifts in a better cause than for carrying on the work thus auspiciously commenced.

Dr Cochrane, as Dean of the College, has received applications from over two hundred young men desirous of becoming students. As a stiff matriculation examination has to be passed, only the very best have been accepted and the work begins with a class of over fifty.'

When all the formalities, speeches and congratulations were over, visitors eagerly embarked on a tour of inspection throughout the building. They examined every nook and cranny, all the equipment, and ended up in the library where tea and cakes were being served by the ladies of the Mission.

A week after the day of celebration, College work began. The young students began their training full of enthusiasm and purpose. Their course for the first year's study included Anatomy, Physiology, and Histology, with a separate course in Biology and Practical Zoology.

And then Tom had a really frightening experience. He only dared to speak of it years later: '*I was making my rounds for the night to see that patients in the hospital were comfortable and that students in the dormitories were attending to their studies, when I saw a red glow, as of a fire, reflected on the window of a cellar. My suspicions were aroused and I crept softly down the cellar stairway, and this is what I saw in the dim, smoky light. In the middle of the floor there was a large, white clay stove in which the Chinese burn balls of mixed clay and coal dust. On the top of these burning balls rested a big enamel basin. Standing over the basin was a Chinese student in his long, black gown, down the back of which hung the then non-discarded queue. I crept silently nearer, and to my horror saw that, with a pair of chopsticks he was turning round and round in boiling water, a human head! I sprang forward and faced him, the boiling head between us, and, aghast at my discovery, he confessed there and then that, in the interests of his studies, osteological specimens being few, he had gone outside the city to a graveyard and found one of the too numerous, scarcely covered, flimsy coffins of the kind which the Chinese describe as "dog-hits-it-with-its-head-and-breaks-it", and had severed a head from a body, brought it stealthily back and was boiling off the flesh*!'

It was to be several years before the Government of China – and then it was the Government of the Republic and not of the *Manchu* Dynasty – allowed the body of a criminal to be dissected at the Kiangsu Provincial Medical School in Soochow. This occurred on November 13th, 1913, and it was stated that this was the first dissection performed in China in four thousand years. In June 1914, the Minister of Education issued an edict authorising dissection in the medical schools of the unclaimed bodies in the jails. The PUMC was amongst the first to apply to the Government and received three bodies. As the Edict had come very suddenly, as it was very hot weather and no preparations had been made for the preservation of bodies, it was necessary for a time to refuse other bodies that were offered, which caused considerable confusion. The chief thing was that the custom of *four thousand years* had been broken and there was no reason to believe it would ever again block the path of scientific medicine in Peking.

Back in 1906, however, teachers of Anatomy were still toiling away with bones, slides, plates, and other second-hand paraphernalia which could never take the place of dissection. All sorts of devices were resorted to, including the use of old articles of clothing, which were made to represent various hollow organs of the body, thereby enabling the would-be surgeons to understand how such organs might be repaired. In Peking, even a Professor of Medicine at the College was goaded into saying that Peking was 'a specially difficult place to study medicine as one got temperate, tropical and local diseases all together, and no post-mortem to help.'

During the whole of this period, the Grand Eunuch continued his private visits to Tom's house and took a lively interest in all that went on in the medical scene. After the official opening, Li Lien Ying was not slow in jogging the Empress-Dowager's memory and at extracting favours for what he no doubt considered in part his 'baby' – the College. The two men became very friendly and Tom never saw nor experienced for himself anything of the dark side of Li's nature. On the contrary, he was undeviatingly helpful and encouraged Tom frequently to make representations to the Throne.

Tom sent a copy of the curriculum to the Minister of Education, asking for degrees to be conferred upon the students. This showed that the teaching and examining staff was representative of the Union of missionary forces which had made the College possible. It also gave the names of the Examining Board, which included medical men from some of the Legations in Peking – British, American, Italian and others.

This recognition was implemented by the bestowal of diplomas of the Board of Education. Another interesting result was that the Government adopted, word for word, the curriculum of the College as a model for any Government Medical College of the future. The final stages were that several Government Boards gave annual grants for the upkeep of the College.

And then suddenly, after one of the Grand Eunuch's midnight visits, Tom was invited to an Imperial audience in the Palace, ostensibly to return thanks for the Empress-Dowager's benevolence.

His own account is graphic –

'*As far as I know, I am the only missionary who was ever granted the privilege of standing in front of the Dragon Throne. The scene was one of oriental splendour and dignity. The Empress-Dowager sat enthroned. She looked every inch a queen, and supported with a quiet and splendid dignity a position which a long line stretching back to the beginning of history – a line of over two hundred monarchs – had occupied before her.*

On her left, but on a lower level, sat the Emperor, who was now but a puppet, with a bored and amused look on his face, not untinged, one imagined, with a sense of shame and humiliation. Princes and high officials kotowed in her presence, and the great Prince Ch'ing on his knees presented an address. Some of the two thousand Palace eunuchs, many of whom, from the powerful Head Eunuch downwards, had been my patients, were in "trembling attendance." In the background were some of the ladies-in-waiting of the Empress, dressed in robes of such beauty as was seldom rivalled by any other nation.

Looking back on that scene, historically so suggestive, and picturing the marble boat, the camel-backed bridge, the Palace buildings, with their yellow-tiled roofs supported upon massive, artistically painted beams, and the lovely setting of the whole on the Jade Lake at the feet of the pagoda-crowned hills that look up to the Western Mountains, I wondered – and have often wondered – that the Chinese allowed the whole rich pageant to pass away with so much unconcern. They, and the world, are poorer for the loss of living, acting representatives of a great past of unique interest. A constitutional monarchy retaining the Imperial glories of ancient China might have bound the great Empire together in a progressive march.'

In another account, however, Tom reveals a different impression made on him. As he stood, a quiet, plain figure dressed in black in front of the Dragon Throne, his eyes downcast as Prince Ch'ung's speech of thanks on his behalf was read, his attention became riveted on the carpet. It was a European carpet of hideous design and inferior texture, totally out of place in the beautiful oriental Throne Room, where everything Chinese was of the very best.

The contrast caused by this inharmonious arrangement gave Tom such an aesthetic shock that he later used it as an illustration of the inappropriateness of a Republic being introduced into the nation, which was out of keeping with the Imperial glories of ancient China. 'But,' as he also later remarked, 'These are matters with which foreigners, and especially missionaries, have nothing to do.'

However, thoughts such as these could not be shaken off easily. When Tom returned home late that afternoon, he went into the bedroom and shut the door. He needed to be alone. The larger house in which they now lived had a beautiful garden, which the window of his bedroom overlooked. As he gazed out over the trees and the flowers, a deep dissatisfaction seized him. For all the pomp and ceremony of the day, the honour and distinction of being summoned and received by the Empress-Dowager, the congratulations of friends, he felt an emptiness. Something was wrong; something was missing. He realised that Tzu-Hsi had never looked at him directly. Why should that hurt? Did she ever look anybody full in the face? It was only a few years back that she gave audience only from behind the yellow curtain and those on the other side heard only her voice. Today she had not spoken. As he thought about it, he realised that the source of his disappointment lay in his failure to be able to communicate with her personally; he had merely had to stand silently while someone else knelt at her feet to convey his thanks. There was that in him which desired always to use his personality to draw others to him in a one-to-one relationship of love and truth and reality. He longed to penetrate the mask behind which the Empress-Dowager lived. He longed to impart to her something of his own love and yearnings for China. He could not believe that she was a happy woman. The sight of the young Emperor, subdued and totally humiliated, relegated to a position almost at her feet, made him wonder if a greater good for China would not have been brought about by the single conversion of this loveless tyrant, rather than the establishment of a dozen medical training colleges in China.

It was a further deep irony that he had been received because of his services and usefulness to China in bringing modern scientific knowledge from the West – yet she had imprisoned, punished and stripped of all authority her young nephew who had tried, as Emperor, in 1898 to encourage the same sort of projects. Tom wondered if the incongruity of this thought had occurred to her during the audience. He wondered again about the carpet. Who had put it there? Was it intended as a subtle insult on her part to bring home the inferiority of the West in contrast to the East? Or was it a clumsy effort to make some sort of acknowledgment to the West, and a sop to a foreign nationality? If so, then it brought no credit to the taste or the products of Western manufacture.

Tom shook himself mentally. What was wrong with him? On this day, of all days, he should not be full of anxious doubts. He should be rejoicing and exuberant with his family and friends at the way his prayer to touch the Dragon Throne had been answered. Yes, God had answered his prayer, marvellously, almost miraculously, yet so naturally that the results of that 'touch' were tangible, real aids to China. It was Tzu-Hsi herself that worried him. Had he touched her heart? An equal part of his prayer had been to turn her heart to Christ. Well, there was still time. This might be just the beginning of some new process. He would still hope and pray for her.

It was growing dark as he stared out into the trees and the brilliant picture of the Dragon Throne, the ladies-in-waiting in their gorgeous robes, the eunuchs all in trembling attendance and the Princes grouped around the Throne, gradually faded from his consciousness. As the light faded, he felt as if he were being projected forward in time. He could still see the Dragon Throne, but now the great Throne Room itself was empty and silent. Then it seemed to him that a throng of people, mostly young people, gay and curious, filled the room, examining the furniture, gazing at the works of art, laughing, amused. All the dignity and splendour had vanished and there was no sign of a European carpet on the floor. As darkness took over and Grace came gently tapping on the door, that picture also faded. Tom came back to himself, as he answered Grace's enquiry through the door and said he would be downstairs in a minute. What had happened to him? Had he been given a preview of the future? What would happen to China – and to medicine, education and religion – if the Empire were to dissolve? What use then would it be to have been allowed to 'touch the Throne of China'? He was troubled as only a brilliant achiever can be troubled, not knowing exactly what had been achieved. He could not, even in his most wakeful moments, see the young Emperor ever being in a position of authority, or exercising the great and beneficent power of many of the late Emperors who had ruled so successfully over the whole of the vast Chinese Empire. In distress, he reached for his Bible, turning the pages to the Psalms. He needed reassurance on this day of triumph and vindication. He found, and slowly read, *Psalm 118*:

v 5 – '*I called on the Lord in distress;*
The Lord answered me and set me in a broad place.'
v 6 – '*The Lord is on my side;*
I will not fear.
What can man do to me?'

v 7 – '*The Lord is for me among those who help me;*
Therefore shall I see my desire on those who hate me.'
v 8 – '*It is better to trust in the Lord*
Than to put confidence in man.'
v 9 – '*It is better to trust in the Lord*
Than to put confidence in princes.'

He closed the Bible, and went down to Grace.

14

Death of the Dragon

About two years after their arrival in Peking, the Cochranes had moved out of their little box-like Chinese quarters into a larger and far superior house within the London Missionary Society's compound, to which there was a walled area at the entrance, a gateway and a porter's lodge. Within the walled area there were three houses, a tennis court and an artesian well, which supplied them with drinking water. Beyond the wall was what later became a womens' hospital.

The house was built of brick, with a slated roof. There were three bedrooms and a spare bedroom, two *en suite* bathrooms, but no tap water. Bath water had to be carried in buckets upstairs. Downstairs were a drawing-room, a dining-room and a study for Tom. There was a large storeroom, in which were kept supplies of tinned foodstuffs from England, and other things sent out annually, which were unobtainable in China. Tinned butter and milk were essentials. There was of course a kitchen with a Chinese brick stove and large Chinese water butts.

The Cochranes counted themselves fortunate in that they had what was virtually an indoor privy, from which the night soil was removed by access from outside every night. There was also a yard containing quarters for the Chinese staff, who fed themselves. The domestic staff consisted of a cook, a houseboy and a coolie. The house was partially centrally heated from a furnace in the cellar which distributed hot air. They owned a modified Chinese cart – later to be emblazoned with Imperial colours – a mule and a groom.

This change from the primitive quarters in which they had lived, in Chaoyang first, and later in Peking itself, coincided with the development of Tom's contact with the Imperial Palace, his appointment as Medical Adviser to the Imperial Maritime and Customs Service, and his various appointments to the British and other Legations. He had by then also acquired many patients of high official standing, and this necessitated a 'social competence'.

For all this, Tom still cared for his 'Peking beggars' at the dispensary, as well as the three other dispensaries he had opened around the city. When it was called for, he still shared his own food with them.

Tom Cochrane, younger of the twin sons, recalls those days in Peking –

'Our standard of living was such as to be found amongst a well-established professional class of the Edwardian era at home. This was possible because everything in China was cheap . . . but there was always the threat of disease – smallpox, epidemics of cholera, typhoid, typhus, intestinal fevers, malaria, tropical sprue, etc., as well as the diseases occurring at home. The mortality and morbidity rate was high amongst missionaries and mother kept an eagle eye on hygiene. We had no amah; *mother took care of her children herself and this no doubt accounted for our good health. The climate was extreme, 110 Degrees Fahrenheit in summer and probably minus 20 Fahrenheit in winter. Canals and rivers froze. Ice was obtainable throughout the summer because the Chinese hewed large blocks of ice in the winter and stored them in strawlined pits.*

When Edgar was about seven years of age he went to a boarding school in Tiensin. The American parents there complained because their children learned to speak American with a Scottish accent! Edgar hated this school, as he hated being at boarding school in England. Bob and I did not go to school until we returned from China and were by then nine years old. We did have some instruction from mother, but we were at least one year behind. In the early summer, we went off to the Western Hills to a bungalow and spent the hot months there in comparative comfort. The bungalow was built in an area which contained many houses which had belonged to the British Legation and were destroyed by the Boxers and never rebuilt. Father was a workaholic and remained at work when all other Europeans were on vacation. He used to come out to the hills which were a day's journey, or for two or three days at a time. We returned from the hills in early autumn.

As children, we had rather an isolated life, as there were no other children on the compound and the other LMS *missionaries were unmarried. We did not mix with the Chinese for a variety of reasons. Contact on a social level was hardly possible because of the difference in standards, culture, hygiene, etc., and in any case the well-to-do Chinese did not embrace Christianity, nor did they want to associate with foreigners. Mother entertained visiting missionaries, visitors interested in missionary work and those especially interested in Father's schemes and projects. The house was nick-named "The Hotel." Mother also helped in the Womens' Hospital (built in 1907), but I believe that her limited proficiency in Chinese was a handicap. The fact that Father was consulted by the nobility of high rank, government officials and by the Empress-Dowager's nephew and trusted by them was really a wonderful achievement. He had a charismatic personality defined as an ability to persuade . . . I sometimes wonder whether the "Old Buddha" ordered her Chief Eunuch and other members of her Court and Government to seek Father's advice acting as guinea-pigs! Father became an excellent Chinese scholar and worked hard to master the roots and construction of Chinese characters, in order to be able to create new characters for anatomical teaching.'* (It was said of him by one Chinese friend that if there were five men talking Chinese in a room and one of them was Tom Cochrane, it would be impossible to know which one was the foreigner!)

However that may be, and however much Edgar hated being sent away to school in England, by early 1908 the twins' education and their future had become an urgent problem. Reluctantly and not without much inner pain, their parents decided that they would have to send their sons to England and it was decided to send them to the same school as Edgar, so as to keep the family together. Tom wrestled and strove with the pain of relinquishment very much as Abraham had struggled with God's demands upon him regarding Isaac; in his diary he interpreted the blessing and the promises given to Abraham because of his faith in a directly personal manner. '*In thy seed shall all the nations of the earth be blessed, because thou hast obeyed my voice,*' (Gen 22.18) he quoted, and added, '*This means, my Father, that Thou wilt make it up to my three boys.*'

In November, 1908, the Empress-Dowager died. The Emperor died the day before, a broken young man who had tottered into her presence at the early morning audience and made his final prostration before her. He had known for some time that he was dying and so did she. The story that reached Tom's ears at Court was that, unprecedentedly, that morning, the Empress-Dowager had tears on her cheeks and had told the young man, 'You need not kneel.' His reply had been, 'I will kneel. It is for the last time.'

She, on the other hand, celebrated her seventy-third birthday that day with a boating picnic on the Lake at the Summer Palace and enjoyed a dish of crab apples and clotted cream. Some hours later, she announced that she herself was dying. She had an attack of gastro-enteritis, from which she began to recover and then relapsed. By then she had been informed of her nephew's death. The next day, she had a seizure after lunch. Protestingly, but with bravado, she issued her final Edict appointing yet another three-year old child, Pu-Yi, as ruler of the Empire, though with Prince Ch'un, his father, as Regent. Pu-Yi was her sister's grandson. At the same time, she appointed the Emperor's widow to be Empress-Dowager in her place, thus keeping the occupancy of the Dragon Throne in the family.

This time Tzu-Hsi knew that her summons was a reality and that the time had come for her to 'mount the Dragon and ascend to the Nine Springs'. She did not go either willingly or peacefully and like Elizabeth I of England, who refused to lie down to die and kept her whole Court on its feet for 24 hours, Tzu-Hsi died imperiously, grudgingly and convulsively. As she issued her final commands, 'Obey! – for a myriad years!' she died with her mouth wide open as if loath to stop speaking.

The funeral and burial of the Empress-Dowager and the Emperor were a massive affair, costing the nation something like six million taels. Tom learned from eyewitnesses that his friend Li Lien Ying stumbled along in the procession, a shrunken, wizened-looking old man who had aged twenty five years overnight. The death of his mistress was the death of his career. Whether the death of the Emperor actually lay at his door no-one was ever to know, but when the Empress died, it was as if the life force of this vigorous man was cut off at a stroke.

The change of personnel at Court was so rapid and changes so far-reaching that there were no means at Tom's disposal to pursue the fate of his one-time friend. Only the flower pots and other momentoes he had received from the Grand Eunuch remained as a reminder of the friendship which had had such significance in Tom's life. Li Lien Ying disappeared and nobody ever heard of him again.

Tom and Grace missed all these dramatic and traumatic events for the simple reason that they were on furlough in England getting the twins settled into school and were actually at sea on their return voyage when this happened. They were an unusually muted couple on their way back to China, each feeling the soreness of parting from their children. Tom, as was normal for him, however, was soon considering plans and hopes for the College and his mind was busy with the future. Grace, though already pining for her twins, and thinking how desolate the house would seem, nevertheless faced the coming days with fortitude; one part of her was relieved that she no longer had the anxiety of constantly protecting the children against all the health hazards that existed in Peking. The house would never be 'home' to her again, but she could at least continue to run the 'hotel' efficiently.

When they arrived at Shanghai, the news of the sudden death of both the Empress-Dowager and the Emperor was a violent shock to them. It seemed incredible. '*Both* of them?' exclaimed Grace, 'and . . . on the same day! How can one believe it?' Tom did not reply. He had a strong sense of foreboding; he remembered the vision he had had on the night of his appearance before the Dragon Throne. What would happen to China now? He felt an intense sadness about the Empress-Dowager herself. He had prayed for her consistently, but had never seen any significant change of heart in her. She had continued to send patients to the Hospital regularly over the last two years, but always with the proviso that they could receive treatment from the Western doctors, but on no account were they to listen to any religious teaching. Christianity was banned at Court. It was not even to be discussed. In his own heart, Tom had always nurtured the hope that eventually the Empress would be reconciled to her nephew, whose life had been literally a martyrdom ever since she had had him stripped of all power in 1898. If he had survived her . . . the thought that Li Lien Ying might have had something to do with the timing and sequence of the deaths thrust itself at him. *If* the Emperor had survived the Empress, even if only by a day, then Li Lien Ying's life would not have been worth a 'cash'.

Many times in the future, Tom was to wonder if the Grand Eunuch would have confided in him if he had been in Peking at the time of the royal deaths. He would never know, for Li Lien Ying had got out of Peking and was gone without trace. Perhaps, thought Tom, when the shock abated, it was just as well. Li had never dissembled with him, and for Tom to be put into the role of confessor would have made life extremely difficult if not dangerous. Despite the unpopularity and bitter hatred that the Grand Eunuch had engendered at Court and with all those who had had business dealings with him, Tom knew him only as a patient and a man, if one could call a eunuch a man. To Tom he had revealed only the problems of a eunuch, a genuine gratitude and an attitude of friendship; his admiration and loyalty for the Empress-Dowager amounted to an obsession.

As soon as the Cochranes arrived back in Peking, Tom was swallowed up in the life of the College; not entirely swallowed up, however, for by now the missionary in him was beginning to take precedence over the doctor. He was still Principal of the College, but was beginning to realise that he and his fellow missionaries did not always see eye to eye regarding the missionary side of their work. The country was in a state of upheaval. The *Manchu* dynasty was beginning to crumble and was going to collapse. Tom still attended Palace patients, Prince Su and Grand Councillor N'a T'ung were still his very good friends and he was more than ever in demand with the wealthy and official Chinese classes and with the Legations, including the British. But he felt that with the death of the Empress-Dowager and the Emperor, the foundations on which the College had been built could be shaken. Life went on in Peking, but not quite as before. More and more Tom heard news of student unrest, the resurgence of rebellious movements, the activities of Sun Yat Sen. Sun Yat Sen was a young Cantonese revolutionary who claimed to be a Christian. He had now taken up residence in Japan, where all the reformers had gathered who had been thwarted in the earlier Reform Movement, and their determination was to bring down the *Manchu* dynasty once and for all. If there were a Revolution, what would happen to the voiceless millions of the Chinese people? Tom wondered. More and more he revolted against the sectarian nature of the Christian churches, so irrelevant to the needs of this nation struggling towards a new era. He countered this by appealing for a federation of the multiple missionary societies and succeeded in setting up an 'Advisory Council for China'; he obtained sponsorship from the LMS to direct and try to co-ordinate all their work, medical and educational and still be in direct contact with, and be funded for the PUMC, by the Government if possible. His great prayer and hope was to create a Christian climate all over China and all over the earth. He was saddened that amongst the British diplomatic class, there did not appear to be any who made an active Christian profession, or seemed to care about bringing Christ to China. The burden, therefore, was all the more weighty on the missionaries, who might eventually face total evacuation. At the instigation of the LMS, who had set up an administration centre in Shanghai, he began to travel widely, visiting missionary stations both of his own Mission and of others. Tom now had more opportunity for speaking and preaching and for advising on the direction that mission work should take.

Shortly before and during 1911, two major events occurred. One was a fearful epidemic of pneumonic plague, which started in Manchuria, raged in Harbin and then hit the north of China in December, 1910. The Chinese Government sent doctors from the PUMC to suppress it, but the situation worsened. In the New Year, the Foreign Office called a meeting of all doctors in Peking to discuss plans to prevent the Plague spreading into Chihli, the province in which lay Peking. This meeting was held in the College, and the Foreign Office appointed the College as the distributing centre for Plague vaccine, commissioning it to order large supplies of disinfectants and disinfecting apparatus.

The PUMC report for 1910-11 states –

'Then came news that the quarantine regulations for Chihli had been enforced too late – Plague had appeared south of the Great Wall. Next a case occurred in Tientsin; two of our graduates and thirteen of the senior students volunteered for duty there. A few days later a man was brought to our hospital in the evening, and died the next day at noon. The symptoms were very suspicious, and after a microscopic examination of the blood, our doctors were able to demonstrate the presence of the Plague bacillus. With this positive proof it was possible to move the authorities to close and disinfect the focus of infection – an inn in the Southern City – and to isolate all contacts.

The City was divided into a number of sections and a large number of sanitary inspectors were appointed. Every case of death was investigated and no coffin could be bought without a certificate from the sanitary authorities. Ten of our graduates were engaged by the Home Office for the supervision of this work in Peking, and so thorough was their work that in two or three weeks the Plague in Peking was stamped out.'

Regretfully, two of the senior students succumbed to the disease and died, one of them the most brilliant student in the College and a 'man of most beautiful Christian character'.

Saddened as he was, Tom saw some good results coming out of this. The untimely death of a fellow-student drew the remaining students closer together in their loyalty to one another and heightened their individual sense of responsibility to the Chinese people. At his death, several students consecrated their lives openly to Christian service and others volunteered to speak in the hospital chapel. It also seemed to set a fresh seal of acceptance and approbation on the College by the Chinese Government, who had turned to the PUMC both for guidance and practical help. Could any Government so beholden to a body of men, even if they were foreigners, turn against them or disown them in the future? Tom began to breathe a little more easily, especially when he found the College's part and sacrifice in putting down the Plague was becoming known throughout China.

The other major event of 1911 was that the young Emperor abdicated on the advice of the Regent, his father, and of the young Empress-Dowager who said she could not, just for the sake of her family, bring misery upon an entire people. This followed on the discovery of a revolutionary plot in which province after province had declared its withdrawal from the administration of the *Manchu* Dynasty. Sun Yat Sen had arrived back in China from the United States, where he had been on a propaganda visit, and was elected temporarily President of the Chinese Republic. Characteristically, he appealed for prayers from the Christian world. His triumph was short-lived, however, and the new Empress-Dowager's Edict went on –

'*I have therefore induced the Emperor*' (who was then six years old) '*to yield his authority to the country as a whole, determining that there should be a constitutional republic. Yuan Shih K'ai*' (he who had betrayed the Emperor Kuang Su in the *coup* of 1898) '*has full power to organise a provisional republican government to treat with the peoples' forces on the methods of achieving unity so that the five races, Manchus, Mongols, Chinese, Muslims and Tibetans may continue together in one Chinese Republic with unimpaired territory.*'

The Times' comment was, '*Some of those who know China best cannot but doubt whether a form of government so utterly alien to Oriental conceptions and to Oriental traditions as a Republic can be suddenly substituted for a monarchy in a nation of four hundred millions of men, whom Kings with semi-divine attributes have ruled since the first dim twilight of history.'*

As for Tom, he could not quite believe it. He saw himself again, standing before the Dragon Throne, amidst all the Imperial splendour, and he could not believe that it had all gone forever.

15

Enter Rockefeller

From the year 1911, in his new appointment as Overseer of missionary administration by the LMS, Tom began to travel extensively throughout China, observing, investigating, and surveying the needs and work of the mission field. In particular, he visited hospitals and out-stations. He found that some districts were served by several Missions, whose work overlapped, while in other sometimes quite large areas, there was no medical or evangelistic work at all. He had come back from his last furlough in England that year a changed man. He was charged with a passion for the missionary methods of St Paul – the planting of indigenous churches which would become self-supporting, self-directing, and self-propagating.

This different and new outlook was the fruit of the experiences of fourteen years as a medical missionary, first in Mongolia, where he was the only doctor in thousands of square miles of territory and his medical work so used up his personal energy that he had to depend on a Chinese evangelist to preach for him; then in Peking where he had been charged with the task of teaching and training Chinese students in Western medicine, under Imperial patronage and with resources gathered from wherever he could find them, which had imposed a massive burden of financial responsibility upon him.

Of his earlier experiences as a missionary, he wrote,

'*A good definition of evangelism is "expert friendship", but we acquiesced in, and followed, the usual conventional methods – methods which hold out no hope of evangelising the world in this or any generation. I thought of the work being directed by me at a head-station and out-stations, all subsidised by foreign money, into which preachers trained at mission expense were to be inducted and supported with foreign funds. In other words, I thought in terms of planting stations with mission money, instead of founding indigenous churches. Progress was limited by financial considerations. I was sowing the seeds of professionalism, of dependence upon non-indigenous instead of indigenous resources . . . Every outgoing missionary should be taught to think indigenously. The missionary who talks about "allowing the natives" to do this, or "forbidding them to do that", should be recalled at once . . . but as a matter of fact, the white missionary is often handicapped by a superiority complex and by the practices and environment from which he has come . . . The missionary's job is not easy; his supreme task is to plant the seed of the Gospel among little groups formed into New Testament churches. This seed, once it is successfully planted, will in due season bear all the indigenous fruits which real Christianity always produces, education, social services, care of the sick and other good works.'*

Tom was indefatigable in his efforts to ram this message down into the hearts and wills of all the missionaries he had dealings with. He frequently warned: 'If we do not amend our ways and reform the pattern of our mission work speedily, the hour will come when Governments will do it for us.' He saw with keen clarity how dependance upon the foreigner could weaken the potential leadership and effectiveness of Chinese Christians. He looked for the day when they would be sufficiently numerous and intelligent to act for themselves along their own natural lines under the guiding hand of God's Holy Spirit. '*Big faith and great consecration are all very well,*' he wrote, '*but we must have thorough knowledge. We need to insist upon and study the science of missions. We ought to gather and co-ordinate and reduce the best we have in all books on missions to certain definite principles and practices, and so ensure more successful work and a great return for time and money and men expended.*'

Another point he made was that, 'Knowing Christ better than our predecessors, we ought to love him more and the ardours of our love will impel us to do the greatest possible for him.'

His enthusiasm was so strong that one day one of his fellow missionaries remarked to another, 'Here we are. In each station we have an LC (Local Committee); then over that a DC (District Committee); and then in our Shanghai headquarters an AC

(Advisory Council); and over and above all, TC (Thomas Cochrane).'

But for all his love of co-ordination and organisation, Tom never lost sight of the fact that each person in the world was a human being, loved of God distinctly from all other individuals and of priceless value. He was ever on guard against thinking in terms of masses of human beings, or of developing a 'mass movement' mentality. His vision had always been world-wide and he feared that too many missionaries had a 'funnel vision' and could only see one tiny spot and objective which they had picked out for themselves, while remaining blind to all else. He himself had not chosen to go to China but had simply asked to go where there was the greatest need. He realised now, from the Mongolia adventure, that there was an urgent need for an intelligent and knowing deployment of missionary forces. 'The work cannot be done by a flying column,' he said, 'it is a long and arduous campaign and a wide view and the most careful planning are necessary.' Some of the missionaries he thought of as being sheep with no sense of direction or purpose, and he sought to shepherd them firmly and inexorably to find the will and purpose of God in their lives, as he expected them to do in their turn for the Chinese under their care. He sometimes met resistance, but men knew him as an experienced and thoughtful medical missionary.

If younger men, newly out in China, showed any sign of the white man's superiority complex, Tom would quote the late Empress-Dowager's diatribes and could repeat almost word for word what she had said about missionaries –

'They inoculate our people with the virus of Christianity and the Christian Chinese immediately lose all respect for our laws and customs. Most of the trouble in inland China is caused by Christian Chinese. They refuse to honour their rulers and the lesser officials set over them by these rulers, and all because of the teaching of foreign barbarians who would probably have plenty of reforming to do at home if only they were less prying, less eager to carry nonsensical religious doctrines to other countries, intent on forcing them upon the people of these foreign countries, whether or not those countries approve. And we let them come here because we are more polite than they!'

Although Tzu-Hsi was now forever silent and there was officially a Republic, Tom warned the younger missionaries, especially those newly arrived from England, that the Empress-Dowager's ideas still lived on in many hearts and places in China and that the only way they could hope to win the Chinese to Christ was by way of prayer, humility and service of the 'feet-washing' kind. He still felt that medicine and healing were the prime channels through which to convey the love of God to the Chinese, because this was where their greatest need lay, and their greatest point of receptivity. So he encouraged the small hospital, the struggling dispensary in country districts where there was positively no other help available; and the larger institutes mushrooming in Shanghai, Chansa, Hankow, Nanking, Canton, Soochow. Many of the latter had taken their lead from the PUMC and had embarked on four- or five-year training courses for Chinese students. All mission hospitals were short of funds, and few had any reliable income, the doctors serving the Hospital and living only off their mission salaries which were always small. Money for building or enlarging premises or for equipping with new plant could be raised only by local subscription or by unexpected gifts from home. Somehow the hospitals subsisted off private patients and the tiny contribution the poorer people could pay if they could pay anything. Research work was out of the question. Even the PUMC did not have the facilities for this.

And then, in the spring of 1914, when England was preparing happily for a season of cricket and good living, the United States of America suddenly rolled up its sleeves, and decided that it had a purpose to fulfil in China.

The Charter of the Rockefeller Foundation stated that the purpose of the Foundation was that '*of receiving and maintaining a fund or funds and applying the income and principal thereof to promote the well-being of mankind throughout the world*'. The particular purpose in mind was to form a '*China Medical Commission*' and *its* purpose was '*to enquire into the conditions of medical education, hospitals, and public health in China*'.

Having returned to Peking in a hurry because he had been informed through the American Consul that the PUMC would be one of the first institutions to be examined by the Rockefeller Commission, and as he was still Principal Emeritus of the College, Tom found a great air of expectancy both in medical and official circles.

Yuan Shih K'ai was in the full flush of his career as President of the Republic, and, if not quite on the Throne yet, he was well on his way to it: he was about to propose himself as Emperor of a new Dynasty. The United States was the only one of the Great

Powers so far to have acknowledged his Government, and he could not afford to let an opportunity such as now presented itself slip away. He knew that money poured in from America to help medical education would be popular with both the new student class and with the common people who had not the means to have medical treatment apart from the foreign mission hospitals.

Consequently, in late April 1914 the Commission from New York was received by the President of the Republic of China, entertained to dinner by the Vice-President, and was able to meet important officials. The members of the Commission stayed on in Peking until May 14th, studying the situation there and in Tientsin, in regard to both hospitals and medical training schools. Then they split into two parties, moved on and covered the whole country, including Hong Kong.

The Commission visited altogether seventeen medical schools and ninety-seven hospitals. These included a few Chinese Government-run hospitals and medical schools and Japanese-run hospitals, but by far the majority were missionary medical schools in varying locations and at different stages of development.

On health conditions in China, the Commission's Report said that there could be no doubt that the death rate in the Republic was higher than in any other known country, but it had been said by some Chinese that, taking things as they were, a high rate was not on the whole undesirable. There were too many people in the country, the population was increasing too rapidly, the pressure on the means of subsistence was excessive, and a diminution of the population caused by widespread disease, whether pestilence or otherwise, was on the whole a benefit.

It was not revealed exactly who had said these things, but the outraged American Health Visitors went on, '*Aside from any humanitarian bearing, it must be noted that there is here ignored the enormous importance of the economic effects of widespread disease. If a nation is healthy and efficient, it will be able to greatly increase its productive power from an economic point of view.*' The Report then went on to an enthusiastic appreciation of the vast, untapped resources of China, its unmined metals, deposits of coal, iron, copper and other valuable products. The system of railways already under way would, with the opening of mines, offer a large outlet for labour. Restriction of the numerous rivers of China from devastating annual overflows would also provide another source of labour and would at the same time reclaim areas of valuable agricultural lands. A lowering of the birth rate was also mentioned as being of special importance to China.

Moving on to the subject of Public Health, the Commissioners stated that so far, no Chinese Government, whether central or provincial, had been able to take comprehensive measures for public health. Smallpox was considered by people as a matter of course, leprosy and tuberculosis raged unchecked. Isolation hospitals for contagious diseases hardly existed so far as the Government were concerned.

With a sudden change of tone, the Report switched to the matter of the ravages of the pneumonic Plague in the years 1910-11, not only in Manchuria and China, but threatening other countries as well. It mentioned the Plague Prevention Service which had been the outcome of this and also took the bright point of view that during the epidemic, the Government allowed autopsies, and thus paved the way for the ultimate Edict in 1913 by which autopsies and dissection were officially recognised. It also conceded that in Nanking the Government had recently issued proclamations and posted them throughout the city, saying that all soil carriers must have lids over their buckets; that there must be no defaecating on the streets; that public toilets must be emptied every day; that butchers selling chopped meats must provide screens to protect the meats from flies; and that if any question regarding public health arose in the minds of the people the Governor would be very glad to hear them.

In over one hundred pages of closely analysed observations regarding every institute visited, with details of its housing, staffing, academic facilities, etc., the recommendations of the Commission were that the first medical educational work organised by them should be in the City of Peking and that it should be in connection with the Union Medical College.

Not only was the College selected because of its location – Peking was considered by far the most suitable place, being the seat of Government, and easily within reach from all parts of the country, but it had the great advantage, as well as being the first in the field of all missionary training colleges, of being recognised by the Government, a privilege not enjoyed by any other missionary school in China.

The Report referred again to the Plague epidemic of 1911, underlining the fact that both professors and students had done the most useful and heroic work, and that this had still further strengthened the College's position vis-à-vis the Government. '*It receives a considerable annual contribution from various Government offices, mainly in return for services rendered by its professors, and some years ago was even honoured by a present from the Empress-Dowager . . . and its inclusion in Peking University, now being planned, will remedy some of its present defects in its organisation. For all these reasons the Commission felt that it was most important that a strong medical school should be maintained at Peking, and . . . that the very creditable beginning made by the missionary societies, and their experience, should be utilised by assisting their institution instead of founding a new one.*'

Tom received a preview copy of the Report privately. With his usual prescience, he had known for weeks what the outcome of the Rockefeller Foundation's Commission was likely to be. He had already faced, in his hours of quiet, what he himself should do. He looked back over his life in China, the three years' horrendous struggle in Mongolia, alone, unsupported and in constant danger. The only visible outcome of those years of hard effort – to think he had once thought of evangelising the whole of Mongolia in one generation! – was one fully qualified Chinese doctor – Liu-i. He moved on mentally to Peking, re-lived his prayer to touch the Throne, his Imperial connections and the establishment of the PUMC. He remembered all the high-born who had begged for his assistance, many of them of noble rank, including princes and dukes and duchesses. He remembered the beggars who had thronged his dispensary day and night, the many operations he had performed in incredibly difficult conditions, the many to whom he had given back their sight; the children and the babies whose lives he had saved from the neglect and ignorance of their parents. And his own contribution to public health warnings in the cholera epidemic of 1902.

He read through, prayerfully, that part of the Report which dealt with China's untapped resources and potential economic value, remembering the huge lumps of coal he had seen lying about on the surface of the ground in Mongolia's neglected and unknown countryside. Strange, he thought, he had never thought of any one of his patients as needing health in order to benefit the nation's economic good. It had always been, as he remembered it, for the patient's own relief or good. But then, he knew he had always been an individualist, just as he had always thought of the Chinese as being a nation of individualists. He suddenly recalled Mr Heaven exhorting him to wear Chinese clothes, assuring him that God must surely have meant him to be a Chinaman because he was so handsome.

All at once, Tom wanted to cry. He had not cried since – when was it? – the night he was left alone in Chaoyang with his family on the road at the mercy of the Boxers; and then again, in his utter weakness when he was recovering from blackwater fever and was sent back to England, when he had cried for the Chinese Christians and the missionaries who had perished at the hands of the Boxers. Had he really been through all that had happened since he landed on the shores of the Gulf of Peichihli fourteen years ago, for *this*? Was it God's will that his life's work, the result of his appeal to touch the Throne of China and to be able to train the Chinese, a plan so beautifully and adeptly worked out for him, should now be handed over to other hands, to those who did not know China as he did? Was he being unfair, or did he detect just the faintest spirit of the *entrepreneur* in the Commission's analysis of China's resources, and its advice? He checked himself; the Rockefeller Foundation's motto was, '*The well-being of Mankind throughout the world*'. What could be more altruistic than that? Was it not what he wanted himself?

Of course China's natural resources had to be mobilised and utilised for the good of its people and its viability as a nation in a modern world. The Americans were not seeking to take over China's economy, only to help them to develop their medical education. But would it mean that everything in this infant Republic would henceforth have only a material value? If everything was to be measured in terms of economic growth or value, would it not quench the spirit? Carried to its logical conclusion it would mean, ultimately, that every Chinese would owe his or her first allegiance to the State. What use, then, to tell them that God was their Father, as he was the Father of all mankind, and that their first duty and privilege was to love the Lord their God with all their heart and all their soul and all their mind and all their strength? Would such a materialistic attitude not lead to worship of the State and not worship of God? Would it not lead also to an intense nationalism, reviving the contempt and hatred for foreigners, just as it was beginning to die out? He remembered all that the Chinese had suffered of indignity, humiliation, and actual harm by the depredations of foreign nations; the resentment invoked by the annexation of territory by the European powers, including

Britain, the establishment of the Treaty Ports, the foreign Concessions, and the huge indemnities China had been forced to pay after the Boxer Rising, and indeed, other Risings?

China was backward in regard to medical science, hygiene, and self-preservation but in the arts and in ethics she had had a purer and more idealistic concept than many Western nations. He hoped that in throwing off the corruption and tyranny of the later period of the *Manchu* dynasty, China would win through to a new, juster and more equitable society where each individual would remain an individual.

He knew that he did not really have any personal choice. If the PUMC was the Rockefeller's choice to start helping China's health problems with her enormous wealth, he would not and could not, stand in the way. It had after all been one of his main ambitions, before his God, to make the College the finest medical training college in the whole of China, the best in Peking. With the Rockefeller millions, the hospital could be transformed into an advanced training and research centre. They were promising to rebuild it in wholly Chinese fashion and the only stipulation was that training must in future be given in the English language, not in Mandarin Chinese. He remembered Li Lien Ying's look of glee when he had first discussed the matter of training with him on one of his midnight visits, when Tom had given his promise that all teaching should be in Chinese and that the Grand Eunuch could reassure the Empress-Dowager on that point. Everything would now be changed, but Tom conceded to himself that this point of change had already been anticipated, with the professorial staff voting five to four against implementing it immediately. The only point that still troubled him was that patients henceforward would not have the Gospel preached to them in the Hospital. The 1911 Hospital Report had described the lives of several patients that year who had undergone a positive conversion to Christ and who had been taught to pray and had left the hospital totally changed beings. What magnificent qualities the Chinese Christians had! They had proved it in the Boxer Rising. Maybe in the uneasy future which he sensed lay ahead of China they would be called upon to prove it again.

The future! What future? He had that day received an invitation from the Rockefeller Foundation to visit New York to discuss and agree on all matters connected with the proposed transfer of the PUMC to the Foundation. He would accept and he would go; he would also resign his own position so as to give the Foundation a fair deal to mould the College in its own way.

As for himself, he knew from that mysterious inner urging that his God was not forsaking him, but was gently releasing him from one work for another. But where and what?

As Tom Cochrane sat in his house in Peking, it occurred to him that here was a chance to go back to his beginnings in thought, and set his sights afresh. He had not chosen God, but God had chosen him and all that he had ever done was to agree and do whatever he was led to do. He was nearly fifty years old and a little old to start again, but he had a packed lifetime of experience to offer. The whole world lay before him and he could give of that experience to those coming after him who were trying to bring Christ to the nations.

A fresh thought struck him. He rummaged about amongst his books and at last he found it – his first original diary, started on his thirteenth birthday, on Wednesday the 12th of October, 1879. The pages were working loose, but the ink had not faded.

'*God is Love*,' he read. '*He has spared me to see another birthday, which is my 13th. Felt very well in mind today. Got two scarfs, one from Maggie, one from Edgar, a fine cake from my mother. I got three birthday cards sent to me. Growing sleepy. I have vowed myself to be GOD's, with his help, forever.*'

He smiled a little, caressing the cover of the book. '*Two scarfs . . . one from Maggie, one from Edgar*!' '*Maggie . . . and Edgar*!' He looked carefully at the inked-in, looped chain effect around the word 'GOD', and below that, the rope. He was glad to be reminded. He had indeed vowed himself that day to be God's forever, with his help. That help had never failed, though he himself may have done so at times. But his vow still held. He was God's then, and he was God's now, and he would be – forever.

The End

Epilogue

I began to write this book in 1966 – the year of the Cultural Revolution in China, the year I visited the United States for the first time – the year my husband died.

During that year I filled a whole student's notebook with research material in shorthand, after studying the letters and archives at what was then still known as the London Missionary Society, but now is called the Council for World Mission. I read all my stepfather's diaries minutely and all the other material I had inherited. The following year my life changed completely. I went abroad and as I stayed there the idea of writing the book faded completely. I was too busy learning a new language. It was not forgotten altogether, however; the story of my stepfather's life and work in Mongolia and China haunted me and occasionally cropped up in conversation. Then, during the last weeks of my living in the Canary Islands, I came across a book on a top shelf, almost hidden away, in the British Library in Puerto de la Cruz, Tenerife. The title was *Life with the Mongols* by James Gilmour. I doubt whether any other reader had taken the book out – not for many years, certainly. When I realised that the author was the famous missionary to Mongolia whom my stepfather had actually followed, I read it through avidly and with a bit of 'arm-twisting', the Orotava Library allowed me to borrow it and take it back to England on the understanding that I returned it in a year's time. This I did when I went back there on holiday. The book fascinated me. It was written with obvious regard and affection for the Mongols, but with none of the piety one would expect from a lonely pioneer missionary who had lost both wife and child there. After reading it, I felt as if God had touched me lightly on the shoulder.

When I had returned to live in England, I had a strange feeling that somehow, sometime, I still had to write the book. But the difficulty then was that, as far as I knew, all missionaries had been evacuated from China in 1951, or had left voluntarily. Bibles had been burnt wholesale in the Cultural Revolution and no traces of Christianity were left – so one was told. Christians, even surviving members of my stepfather's family, felt that nothing was left of his work in China. About China I had read only what was in the newspapers and it seemed to me that all that my book could ever be was a rather sad little vignette of a life which, for all its heroic and pioneering spirit, had left no trace, and of a mission which ultimately failed. So convinced of this was I that I felt I could not face the amount of work involved in writing what could only have a limited historic appeal.

Then, at the end of 1981, I came across a book called *God's Smuggler to China*. I read it. I was invited to go and hear Brother David, of the 'Open Doors' organisation and author of the book, speak at a Seminar about China in the little village of Chedworth, near Cheltenham. I went. I was allowed the privilege of almost an hour's private conversation with Brother David and I came home knowing that at last I really was going to write the book.

I now knew that there was a 'vibrant, flourishing church in mainland China, isolated, but millions strong' as the book cover describes it. It was known as the 'Persecuted Church' and it needed Bibles desperately. Alongside it, the revived Protestant Church of pre-Communist days, originating in the Three-self Movement, was re-opening churches and being allowed public worship by the Chinese Government, which had restored religious freedom after the death of Mao and was willing to tolerate also the Chinese Islamic Association, the Buddhist Association and even the Catholic Patriotic Association. What the Communists' motive was in allowing this toleration religiously needs to be sought both in their ideology and their more recent history. Despite this, millions of believers today meet in each others' houses and not in a church building. There are men – and women – who have a ministry of preaching and healing, and sometimes performing miracles similar to those described in the New Testament. Their character and customs could be most accurately compared with that of the churches founded by St Paul – the sort of churches Tom Cochrane had foreseen and had wanted to encourage.

The twentieth century has proved even more turbulent in Chinese history than was the nineteenth. The fates and fortunes of Chinese Christians during the decade from 1920 on into the 'eighties would require almost a lifetime of diligent on-the-spot research, and a much longer book. To extrapolate any sort of cohesive pattern of the Christian religion surviving amid the political, military and social upheavals would amount to the unmasking of a history within a history. Moreover, each locality in China would have a different story to tell. In fact, many thousands of Christians who suffered persecution under Mao's rule (particularly when all dissidents of any nature were hounded) were executed, imprisoned or tortured. Many died in prison. But others cracked and some lost their faith; some betrayed fellow Christians and even their own families. All were caught in the political net from which there was no escape. All Christians in China today look back on that time – 1966 to 1976 – with horror and shame. To add to their grief, millions of Bibles were burnt in China during the Cultural Revolution and allegiance to the State was made paramount if a man was to earn his living or educate his children.

It is not surprising that, now that the Communist Government has declared religious freedom and has allowed the re-opening of churches, there are many Christians who feel they dare not trust the Government which has never itself wavered from its atheistic beliefs (or disbeliefs). They fear that once their names and addresses are registered as belonging to a church, they could at any time be rounded up. This maybe particularly applies to those new Christians caught up in the present millions-strong revival. There is also the vexed question of co-operation or non-co-operation with the Government in its aims, which are wholly nationalist and material. Here, there are differing views amongst the churches as to what is spiritually good and healthy to do. Some believe it is a positive Christian witness to co-operate with any Government measures which will improve the lot of one's neighbour and one's country; others consider it a compromise to be seen in agreement with those who deny the existence of God and the meaning of Christ and are working for a kingdom of heaven on earth based on a purely materialistic philosophy. I believe no-one from outside is in a position to judge. The only certainty one has as a Christian is that God is working his purpose out. I would like to quote from a letter to me from the recently retired Bishop of Hong-Kong who was himself on the mainland of China from 1934 onwards and through the 'forties and was in Canton when the Communists took over in 1949 –

'*One cannot really know what the long-term result is going to be; people used to say, "Don't you feel your time in China has been wasted since it ended with the withdrawal of all missionaries?" I could never feel that, for I believe God takes care of results and it happens that in spite of many dark days and sad losses, I have found fellow Christians, former students and colleagues who had come through the storm and are again witnessing to Christ in China. It would have been harder to say that ten years ago; but even then I never felt that God had abandoned China or his Church there.*'

The fact that China boasts an atheist Government, which believes in and preaches only the doctrines of loyalty to the State, self-help and material goals, proves only one thing – not that God does not exist, but that he is not known or sought.

But another fact is that God cannot be pushed out of his own world, and if man attempts to do this, God will come back through another door. The present spiritual revival is no new phenomenon. It has happened again and again all through history, when God raised up special people to activate it.

I sometimes wonder how Tom Cochrane would view the China of today compared with the China of his days in Peking.

He would rejoice, I am sure, at the fact that dire poverty has been abolished, that a Chinese baby born in 1983 has a reasonable expectation of life – 68 years today compared with 35 years before 1949; and that the old terror of becoming ill, so it is said, has disappeared. Killer diseases have been harnessed to cure or prevention and hunger as experienced by his 'Peking beggars' is a thing of the past.

He would also admire the fact that China upholds morality, and that corruption, bribes and selfishness are officially considered as blemishes on society, to be exposed and punished; that family life is encouraged, even if efforts to modify the population are legalised and even demanded. I am sure that Chou-en-Lai and my stepfather would have had much *rapport*, had they been able to meet, and even Mao himself, in exhorting the Chinese to practice 'unselfishness' towards one another would, in that matter at least, have had Tom's favour.

What Tom Cochrane would not like today is the way history

has been re-written by the Chinese with complete disregard for some of the livelier and more creative achievements of the hated Westerners in China, those from which no single selfish motive has been deduced, but were directed solely for China's benefit. Of these, the establishment of the famous PUMC is one example, though there were many others. The trouble with the Communists' attempt to re-write history is that, in denigrating everything originally coming out of the West, they have inevitably thrown out the baby with the bathwater. Tom also would have felt that not all the material benefits in the world could have compensated men for their ignorance of God and the Jesus whom he followed, and he would have longed for China to become not only a prosperous, clever and competitive nation in the modern world, but one great enough to learn the secret of forgiveness for old enemies, consigning their evil deeds to the past, to be forgotten in a new comity and peace.

When I consider the history of the College founded by Tom Cochrane known as the PUMC, I am amazed that more pride is not taken in its story. In its reconstructed state, passing through the Rockefeller hands, then being held by the Japanese before finally coming under communist control, it has been associated over the years with such distinguished names as Bertrand Russell, Professor Black (of 'Peking Man' fame) and Pierre Teilhard de Chardin. Bertrand Russell asserts that he owed his life to the PUMC who provided a serum that killed the pneumococci when he was seriously ill in Peking in 1921. '*I owe them the more gratitude on this point*,' he wrote in his Autobiography, '*as both before and after I was strongly opposed to them politically, and they regarded me with much horror*.' In the latter years of the 'Twenties Peking became a highly organised intellectual centre of cosmopolitan nature. Many Chinese scientific institutions were coming into being, backed by eminent American and European scholars. Apart from Black, there were Andersson, the prehistorian; Sven Hedin, the explorer; Granger and Barbour, the palaeontologists, and others. On Sunday afternoons, Teilhard would go to the Palaeolontology Department of the Peking University and work there till late evenings. Not one of these great men had anything but praise for the blisteringly high standards of the Institutes comprising the University. I doubt whether any of them knew of the origins of the Medical College.

In 1966, I received a letter from a Chinese nurse who had been a staff nurse at the famous Medical College from 1940 to 1942.

She mentioned that there were a number of PUMC trained doctors working in Taiwan, the United States, and in Hong-Kong, and that she had seen several of them recently. Not one of them, she told me, like herself, knew that it was a British doctor who had founded the PUMC, and not the Rockefeller Institute.

I have a certain fantasy based on the authority of my ten-year old grand-daughter, who assured me recently that we would meet people 1,000 years old in heaven. She said that there were great big doors that would be shut and then opened suddenly and then shut again. We would *all see God* – 'but only for a minute' she assured me. In my fantasy, I see four men sitting in a corner discussing China (and all speaking Chinese, of course). One is Bertrand Russell, one is Professor Black, one is Pierre Teilhard de Chardin, and the other is my stepfather. Bertrand Russell will insist that the Chinese are a nation of artists and wits, but that he wished he had had more to offer them when he was with them; Professor Black is still bemused by the antiquity of China and its incipient wisdom and potentiality, Pierre Teilhard de Chardin will see the upward movement of society in China today as part of a spiral movement which has drawn and will draw them closer to God, whom they will at last recognise; and Thomas Cochrane will be planning a great 'welcome home' to the descendants of all those brave souls who loyally stuck to him in Chaoyang, those who listened to him as he tried to heal and preach the Kingdom of God in Peking, and to all those others whom he wanted to reach, but there were too many of them. While saluting those who predeceased him by one thousand years on the one hand, he will be welcoming all those who come after him, on the other – all those who belong to God, and perhaps even, some who barely know him, but want to.

It is my hope that my grand-daughter and I will be allowed to sit with these four, even if it is 'only for a minute'.

Appendix

A Brief Historical outline of China: From Early Days to Our Century

The Dynasties of China:

Chows	*BC 1120/250*
Hans	*BC 200/200 AD*
T'angs	*AD 600/900*
Sungs	*AD 960/1280*
Mings	*AD 1370/1650*
Ch'ings	*AD 1650/1911*

By 2700 BC the Chinese occupied the region in the vicinity of the Yellow River. Where they came from is problematical. The period from that time until 1100 BC may be described as semi-mythical and from 1100 BC, when history becomes fairly authentic, as semi-historical.

'In the Beginning'

The Chinese declare that the world was created out of chaos over three million years ago, that it was created by a first cause, which separated into *yen* and *ying*, male and female, or heaven and earth; that man was then created and thus there came to be a triumvirate of three powers – heaven, earth and man.

The 'Golden Age'

In an initial mythical Golden Age people were never punished because they never transgressed. It was superfluous to lock doors. No anxiety was felt about lost property; it was sure to be found or returned. The filial piety of one of the Emperors who was raised from the plough to the throne was so great that even the wild beasts were attracted to him and came to drag his plough.

Early History – the *Chow* Dynasty (1122–250 BC)

History in a fairly authentic sense began with the *Chow* dynasty although the Chinese had already been enjoying some degree of civilisation prior to then. The art of writing was known, astronomical observations had been made, music and painting were cultivated, spirit had been distilled and silk and other materials were used for clothing.

When the *Chows* rose to power China was a federation clustering round a central state. This Central State seems to have managed the affairs common to all, but each principality enjoyed a certain amount of home rule. It was indeed a sort of feudal age, the heads of the various states owing allegiance to the Sovereign, until at the end of nine centuries one of the states, that of *Ch'in*, became powerful enough to defy the others, overthrow the *Chows* and seize the throne, which it held for a period of 50 years, when the *Han* dynasty began.

Religion, politics and medicine

Religious observances were added to in the course of the *Chow* dynasty. The worship of heaven and earth was continued but in addition, dead heroes and natural objects were deified. Ceremonial observances in this period were added to and occupied a very prominent place in official circles. Laws were excessively severe and punishments very barbarous. Before the close of this dynasty the system of regulating affairs without appeal to the higher authorities was inaugurated, by grouping families and appointing elders. A ninth part of the produce of the soil was reserved for the government, coins were cast, and customs duties imposed.

Numerous warlike instruments were invented and chariots were used during this dynasty. The ears were cut off from the bodies of the slain on the battlefield. Slavery was a domestic institution and slaves were sometimes interred alive with the body of a ruler.

During this dynasty medical classification was attempted, linking seasons with specific diseases –

Spring	headache and neuralgic affections
Summer	skin diseases
Autumn	fever and agues
Winter	bronchitis and pulmonary affections

Drugs too were arranged under five classes: those derived from herbs, trees, living creatures, minerals, and grains. Those having *sour* properties were supposed to nourish the bones; *acrid*, the muscles; *salt*, the blood vessels; *bitter*, general vitality; *sweet*, the flesh. The public were safeguarded by a warning against rashly swallowing prescriptions of physicians whose family had not been three generations at least in the medical profession.

Culture

Music was developed to such an extent that Confucius once claimed that certain melody had affected him so deeply that he was not able to taste meat for three months.

The beginning of the art of writing is hidden in the obscurity of the centuries, but certainly by 800 BC it had attained to a state of considerable advancement; the Stone Drums in Peking almost certainly belong to that dynasty.

About the middle of the *Chow* Dynasty the philosopher Lao-Tzu was born, but his system of philosophy gradually became mixed with alchemistic research and Buddhism. He was followed by Confucius, who in turn preceded Mencius.

The *Book of Changes*, the most ancient book in the Chinese language, probably dates from the beginning of the *Chow* dynasty. It deals with a philosophical system based upon combinations and permutations of sets of lines varying in length, representing powers in nature. The *Book of Ritual* came next, and then the literary activities of the later years.

The *Ch'in* Dynasty (250–200 BC)

The fifty years of the *Ch'in* Dynasty, intervening between the *Chows* and the *Hans*, forms an interesting period. In this short dynasty appeared the so-called 'First Emperor' of a united China from which the old feudal system had been swept away. This emperor is supposed to have colonised Japan. He built the Great Wall, which is about fourteen hundred miles long, twenty-two foot high and twenty foot thick. He burned all books, except those on medicine, divination and agriculture, being determined that literature should begin with his reign, and killed many of the *literati* who refused to obey his commands.

The *Han* Dynasty (200 BC–200 AD)

Under the *Han* Dynasty the Empire made great progress, although there were frequent wars with the Tartars on the north, and the Turkish tribes, especially the *Huns*, on the west. During this Dynasty Yunnan was reduced to subjection and added to the Empire. Buddhism was introduced from India. The philosophy of Lao-Tzu underwent changes. The Jews founded a colony in Honan and a great revival of learning took place; ink was invented and paper made. A history was written. Hsu-Shen compiled the *Shuo Wen*. Many other works were written and Yang, the great scholar and official who is immortalised in the ancestral shrine of the clan *The Hall of the Four Knows* lived and died in comparative poverty.

During this dynasty the written Chinese language and the teachings of Confucius were carried to Japan.

Drama is supposed to have been introduced during this dynasty and was suggested by the following incident – A *Han* Emperor besieged by *Huns* sent a messenger to their leader and offered him a beautiful girl on condition that himself and his people would be allowed to pass unharmed through the lines. The *Hun* leader was suspicious, but on repairing to the foot of the City wall he saw a charming young lady moving about among attendants almost as lovely as herself. The Emperor was allowed to escape, but when the *Hun* general ascended the walls, he found that the beautiful young ladies were puppets moved by strings. Theatricals and Punch-and-Judy shows were thus suggested.

The Transitional Era (200–600 AD)

During the transition period of four centuries between the *Hans* and the *T'angs*, wars and changes were frequent. For a time the Empire was divided into three kingdoms, and small dynasties rose and fell. Christianity was introduced by the Nestorians, and printing from wooden blocks began, but nothing very distinctive and outstanding as compared with other periods is recorded. This was followed by the brilliant epoch under the *T'angs* (600 AD–900 AD).

The *T'ang* Dynasty (600–900 AD)

The three centuries of the *T'ang* dynasty were on the whole years of peace, prosperity and progress, and, just as the northerners delight to call themselves sons of *Han*, so the southerners delight to call themselves sons of *T'ang*.

The reign of Hsi Tsung was an interesting period in this dynasty. This Emperor at first wise and virtuous became later sensual and corrupt.

At the beginning of his reign, in order to discourage extravagance in dress, he caused all his valuable wardrobes to be destroyed by fire. He was an enthusiastic patron of literature, especially poetry. The poems of the *Tang* dynasty amount to nearly fifty thousand different pieces. The modulations or tones of the voice which alter the meaning of words were probably much elaborated during this poetic period.

Buddhism greatly deepened its hold during that time. During Hsien Tsung's reign a supposed bare bone of Buddha was transmitted with great care from India and was received with Imperial honours. This drew a protest from the famous scholar Han Wen Kung, who regretted that the Son of Heaven should stoop to be taught at the hands of barbarians. 'Had Buddha come to our Capital in the flesh' said Han, 'your Majesty might have received him with a few words of admonition, a suit of clothes and a banquet, but his bone . . . forsooth!'

During this dynasty a maternal uncle of Mahomet is said to have introduced Mohammedanism into China, and later Arab soldiers came to quell an insurrection and settled in the country.

The 'Peking Gazette' and the use of paper money were introduced during this Dynasty.

A Short Transitional Period (900–960 AD)

An important transitional period of about sixty years existed between the *T'angs* and the *Sungs* and it was probably about this time that the custom of footbinding was introduced (The *Hakkas*, a race of ancient Chinese stock who probably emigrated from north to south China do not bind the feet).

The *Sung* Dynasty (960 AD–1280 AD)

The nation had by this time settled down to that state of culture and civilisation in which it was found later by Europeans. Most of the things seen in China in the way of tools, household furniture etc., date back at least one to two thousand years.

There was an attempt made during this dynasty to introduce compulsory military service. The *History* of Chu Hsi was produced and a whole host of literary men flourished. A compilation of antiquarian researches in three hundred and forty eight volumes were published; trigonometry and mathematics received some attention. Buddhism and Tao-ism became mutually tolerant although both still nominally existed under the ban of Confucianism. The surnames of four hundred and thirty eight people were collected. Inoculation for smallpox was known, at least from the early days of the dynasty and the first work on acupuncture was published. Towards the latter part of this dynasty the Tartars overran the north and finally the Mongols overthrew them and established a Mongol dynasty. During the rule of Emperor Kublai Khan the Grand Canal linking north and south China was completed and this same Emperor organised a great but unsuccessful naval expedition against Japan.

About this time migration of natives from the north to the south took place and their descendants are the *Hakkas*, hardier and more industrious than the Chinese, some of whom have won literary prizes.

The *Ming* Dynasty (1370–1650 AD)

The founder of the *Ming* dynasty rose from poverty and obscurity to the throne of China. He sought to avoid starvation by entering a Buddhist monastery and then became a soldier of fortune and fought against the Mongols. After defeating them he founded a new dynasty with the capital at Nanking. The third Emperor of this dynasty however transferred the capital back to Peking.

Toward the close of the sixteenth century the Portuguese came to China and obtained a concession in Macao. Possibly the origin of gunpowder in China was due to them. About the same time the

Jesuits came to China and their scientific labours filled the Empire with 'sounds that linger still', and had they been able to agree among themselves, China would probably be today a Catholic country. During this dynasty an encyclopaedia of twenty-two thousand books and over one million pages was published. Four copies were made and only a few incomplete portions remained.

A sudden rebellion overthrew the *Mings*; the Emperor committed suicide. His commander-in-chief was at that time on the frontiers of Manchuria resisting the *Manchu* Tartars; he returned to Peking when he heard of the rebellion but was defeated by the rebels. He therefore returned to Manchuria and enlisted the help of his former foes who, when they came, remained to reign until 1911. One of the items of the negotiations was that 'People should adopt the national costume of the Tartars in every-day life but that they should be allowed to bury their corpses in the dress of the late dynasty'.

The *Ch'ing* Dynasty (1650–1911 AD)

Having come to assist China, but remaining to reign, the *Manchus* were interlopers in China. They introduced the queue, or pigtail, which encountered a great deal of resistance in the south. However, it gradually became the fashion. The southerners tried to oppose it but when they found they could not resist they hid it by wearing turbans. *Manchu* garrisons whose soldiers were called 'Bannermen' occupied positions throughout the country.

Ten Emperors of this line have occupied the throne and passed away. The second Emperor K'ang Hsi reigned for sixty-one years. He was a great ruler, treated the Catholic priests with kindness and availed himself of their services. During his reign, the encyclopaedia *Sacred Edict*, a famous dictionary, and many other books were published. He attempted to stop foot-binding but failed.

In the opening of the nineteenth century Protestant missionaries came to China and Dr Morrison published his famous dictionary.

The Opium War

In the reign of the sixth *Manchu*, Tao Kuang, the so called 'Opium War' took place, whereby the British extracted a Treaty of Commerce and a recognition of natural equality from a nation that had up to then looked upon Westerners as unsubdued savages. Hong-Kong was ceded and five ports were opened.

The fall of the last dynasty

The *Tai Ping* Rebellion shook the *Manchu* dynasty towards the close of Tao Kuang's reign, and Emperor Hsien Feng had not been long on the throne when a second war with foreign powers was caused by the Chinese having disregarded the British flag. New treaties were made, but repudiation of responsibility led to further trouble. The British were not allowed to proceed to the Capital, which was ultimately captured by French and English forces who then burned and looted the beautiful 'Summer Palace'. Hsien Feng fled the country and died shortly afterwards. He was succeeded by T'ung Chih, the son of Tzu-Hsi, the Empress-Dowager. Tung Chih died of smallpox as he attained his majority. His mother chose her husband's nephew as Emperor-Elect under the style of Kuang Hsu. Although officially Emperor, he tried to bring about reforms in education and in military affairs which caused the Empress-Dowager to deprive him of all power and authority. He remained virtually her prisoner, humiliated and deprived, until he died on the same day as she did, in 1908. He was succeeded by his brother's son known as P'u Chi. The latter was never more than a puppet Emperor and abdicated in 1911. Thus ended the *Ch'ing* dynasty, which was in fact the last dynasty of all.